A Humanities Press Book

We are pleased to send you a
complimentary copy of

Robert Griffin.

High baroque culture and
theater in Vienna.
. . . *for review*

We would appreciate two copies of
your review.

Publication date . . . 1972

Price . . .   17.50

HUMANITIES PRESS, Inc.
Publishers & Importers of Scholarly Books
303 PARK AVE. SOUTH NEW YORK 10, N. Y.

High Baroque Culture
and
Theatre In Vienna

High Baroque Culture
and
Theatre In Vienna

by
Robert Arthur Griffin, Ph.D.

HUMANITIES PRESS
New York 1972

Published by
Humanities Press, Inc.
New York, N.Y. 10010

Printed in the United States of America
by Noble Offset Printers, Inc., New York, N.Y. 10003

DEDICATION

To Helen in Cheshire
"Your Naiad airs have brought me home
To the glory that was Greece
and the grandeur that was Rome."

Expression of Appreciation

The writer wishes to express publicly his appreciation to the many people in Europe and in the United States who have contributed to the progress and completion of this historical inquiry.

To Professor George L. Lewis, for his knowledgeable and inspirational counseling.

To Professor Robert B. Sutton and Associate Professor John C. Morrow, for their constructive criticism and encouragement.

To Professor John H. McDowell, who first suggested this research, and to his staff of The Ohio State University Theatre Collection for their help in locating, gathering, and classifying much of the resource material.

To Konrad Zobel for his assistance at Vienna on behalf of The Ohio State University Theatre Collection.

To Mrs. Jane Nolan for her assistance and competent work on the manuscript.

Most of all, to Linda Rose and Karen, my daughters, and to Helen Frances, my wife, for their love, enthusiasm, and support of this research.

Table of Contents

PART II: ARCHITECTS OF VIENNESE HIGH BAROQUE CULTURE

PART III: ELABORATIONS AND MODIFICATIONS OF THE STYLE

List of Figures

List of Plates

Plate

Foreword

Baroque. The very word fires the imagination, tantalizes all the senses, and virtually overwhelms its devotees with an elusiveness that defies definition. Nor has there been wanting any number of brave souls who have been eager to sacrifice themselves to the Scylla and Charybdis of the easy solutions; as, respectively, baroque culture was either to be comprehended as a period of decadence following the fading of the renaissance spirit, or that it was a reactionary and neo-Gothic expression of Counter-Reformation Jesuitism. In either case, the study of baroque culture was seen to be an unprofitable pursuit, as evidenced by the shattering disillusionment of its first explorers. Fortunately, this earlier impression is now being overcome, thanks to more balanced approaches by historians of music, literature, art, and architecture. The present work is an attempt to relate some of the more recent findings to the history of theatre, particularly to what the Viennese scholars call the flourishing of High Baroque opera in Vienna during the Burnacini period.

Perhaps the chief difficulty presented by the striking phenomenon of baroque culture is its great similarity to the sense-realism of our own visually-oriented culture. The massive amounts of printed material and artifacts in any one field are sufficient to humble the more rashly adventuresome scholars. In consequence, the approach I have chosen is structural and analytic. The early chapters seek to view the framework within which baroque culture, generally, developed. Special emphasis is accorded those transitional elements which mark the separation of baroque phenomena from those of the renaissance, and which provide some practical rationale for their occurrence. My reason for stressing the significance of socio-economic factors in theatre art is quite plain; plays cost money, and the production of opera requires even more money, men, and materials. Consequently, art is never irrelevant to its contemporary modes of science and technology. A second, but no less important point in this connection has been to correct the false impression that baroque culture was merely the creation of the princely circles for their private courts; and to underline the well-established thesis of Per Bjürstrom, that *baroque opera in particular was the product of the people,* taking on its most characteristic features in the public theatres of Venice during the first half of the 17th centuries. This point does not conflict with the Florentine origins of early opera; it merely seeks to place the whole development in a more realistic, balanced perspective. On the basis of this foundation, then, an attempt is made to construct an understanding of the growth of High Baroque culture and opera in Vienna during the second half of the seventeenth century.

To give deserved credit to the many persons who have assisted me in this study is not now possible. In a real sense, the results of this book cover more than a decade of study, travel, and research. The book itself might be called a neo-baroque synthesis by a college major in economics, who learned art history in the private circle of artists occasionally gathered at the Aliquippa, Pa., home of Charles Williams; who traveled to Göttingen to study German culture and philosophy under Professor Hermann Wein and logic under Drs. Joseph König and Günther Patzig; and who used his previous gleanings to accomplish a research project at The Ohio State University Theatre Collection. A certain predilection for exegetical and expository writing is traceable to my theological studies concluded at the Pittsburgh Theological Seminary in 1954, where Drs. Jackson, Gerstner, and Theophilus M. Taylor were my most influential teachers.

Special acknowledgment for the results of this study should be given to Dr. George L. Lewis, my very creative advisor at Ohio State, to Dr. John McDowell, who guided the research in seminars at the OSU Theatre Collection, and to Dr. John Morrow, who patiently read and offered many constructive suggestions on the manuscript, especially in regard to its basic format.

Particular credit must be given to Hofrat Dr. Hans Pauer, Director of the *Bildarchiv der Österreichischen Nationalbibliothek* for providing the author with outstanding iconographic materials from the original Burnacini scene designs of *Il pomo d'oro;* and for granting permission to incorporate reproductions of the scenes into the main contents of the book. Other sources to be acknowledged, and from whom permission has been granted for the adoption of textual and illustrative materials, are as follows: the *Bibliothèque et Musée de l'Opéra* of Paris, France; the *Herzog Anton Ulrich-Museum* in Braunschweig, Germany; the *Sächsische Landesbibliothek* in Dresden; the *Germanisches Nationalmuseum* in Nürnberg; and to Professor Per Bjürstrom of the *Nationalmuseum* in Stockholm, Sweden, for permission to quote from his definitive work on Giacomo Torelli. Valuable assistance and permission to quote brief excerpts of passages has also been granted by the following authors and publishers: Harry N. Abrams, Inc., New York; *Akademische Verlagsgesellschaft Athenaion,* Frankfurt, Germany; W. W. Norton & Co., New York, publishers of *Music in Western Civilization* by Professor Paul H. Lang; Almquist and Wiksell, Swedish publishers of Bjürstrom's study on Torelli; Appleton-Century-Crofts, Educational Division, Meredith Corporation, New York, publishers of *The Growth of European Civilization* by Slosson, *et al.,* c. 1943; A. S. Barnes & Co., Inc., New Jersey; Barnes & Noble, Inc., New York; Benjamin Blom, Inc., New York, for use of *Stuart Masques and the Renaissance Stage* by A. Nicol; John E. Bielenberg, SUNY Associate Professor of Theatre at Binghamton, New York, for quotations from his original research on Filippo Juvarra; The Clarendon Press, Oxford, England, publishers of *Venetian Opera in the Seventeenth Century* by Simon T. Worsthorne, 1954; Crown Publishers, Inc., New York; Encylcopaedia Britannica, Chicago, Illinois; Verlag Francke, Bern, Switzerland; Harper & Row, Publishers, New York, publishers of *Economic History of Europe* by Herbert Heaton, and *The Art of Scenic Design* by Lee Simonson; George C. Harrap & Co., Ltd. and Harcourt,

Brace & World, Inc. of London and New York, respectively, publishers of *The Development of the Theatre* by Allardyce Nicoll; Professor John Morrow, Ph.D., Director of Graduate Studies in the Department of Theatre at The Ohio State University, who authored the essay on the OSU Theatre Collection for *Player's Magazine;* the Otto Müller Verlag, Salzburg, Austria, publishers of the monumental *Theatergeschichte Europas* by Professor Dr. Heinz Kindermann of the University of Vienna, to whom I am especially indebted for the excellent materials and insights contained in volumes III and IV; The Philosophical Library, Inc., New York, publishers of *The Rise of English Opera* by Eric W. White; again, to *Player's Magazine* for permission to quote at length from its Nov. '64 article by Dr. John Morrow; Reclam of Stuttgart, Germany, publishers of *Baroque Drama;* Hewitt, Barnard, ed. *The Renaissance Stage: Documents of Serlio, Sabbatini and Furttenbach.* (Rare Books of the Theatre No. 1) Coral Gables, Fla: University of Miami Press, 1959, 3rd prtg 1966. x, 256 pp. Drawer 9088, c. 1958 by University of Miami Press; Verlag Gebr. Mann GMBH, Berlin, Germany, publishers of *Barocktheater und Barocke Kunst* by Professor Dr. Hans Tintelnot; The Ysel Press Ltd., Deventer, Holland, publishers of iconographic materials of El Greco; Simon Silverman, editor for the Humanities Press, Inc., New York, whose over twenty years' experience in publishing has frequently been of great help in the production of the book; and to President Dr. Hilton C. Buley and the Board of Trustees for the State Colleges in Connecticut, whose generous work provisions have made the book possible. Finally, and most notably, credit must be given to the patience of my children, Karen and Linda, from whom time has often been borrowed for the completion of this study; and to Dr. Helen Frances Griffin, Research Associate in Radiobiology & Biochemistry at Yale University, who is also my wife and the masterful conductor of integrated scientific, humanitarian living at the research lab and in the home.

New Haven, Conn.   Dr. Robert Griffin
February 6, 1971

Introduction

The flowering of baroque culture on the European continent following The Thirty Years' War is one of the most remarkable events in Occidental history. The war itself seems to have done little more for Central Europe than to settle the administration of religious problems. In its wake it had consumed eight million people, devastated fields, and broken the power of the new commercial centers, chiefly by destroying them. The landed nobility, who drew up The Peace of Westphalia in 1648, seemed to sense a need for consolidation and the restoration of authority. A time of peace was also needed to allow for the strengthening of such cultural forces as would support the new spirit of absolutism, which was being nurtured to oppose any new attacks from growing commercial centers. Such a peace would also permit the ruling princes to assimilate into Central Europe the newer developments in art and music which the Counter-Reformation leaders had produced in Spain and Italy, principally in Venice.

The one person who more than any other came to dominate the history of theater in Europe during the latter half of the seventeenth century was Ludovico Ottavio Burnacini. While Giacomo Torelli was the celebrated genius of stage machinery in the early part of this period, inadequate support in Paris and Venice did not permit his work to reach maturity. The rising star of the post-Torelli generation was recognized to be the architect of High Baroque culture at Vienna, Ludovico Burnacini.

Statement of the Problem

The historical problem is one of establishing the impact of theatrical performances at the Viennese Imperial Court during the High Baroque period. While the character of this impact is closely intertwined with the economic, social and cultural relationships which accompanied the growth of The Grand Alliance against the designs of Louis XIV, King of France, our main purpose requires the subordination of these ramifications to the actual development and blossoming of baroque theatre at the Viennese Imperial Court. For the sake of understanding the conditions which encouraged High Baroque theatre culture, as well as for an insight into the function of that culture, as seen in its effects, some space is justifiably given to the educational implications of events which occurred in and about Vienna. A knowledgeable history of theatre also implies that real, evolutionary trends of art should be indicated wherever they occur. For this reason, some mention will be made later of L. O. Burnacini's apparent influence on Santurini, architect at Munich, and J. O. Harms, first theatre architect and professional designer in the Northern German states.

Writers on cultural history commonly divide the periods after the Middle Ages according to the titles of renaissance, baroque, and rococo.[1] The last mentioned, which refers to highly ornate furniture and architecture of the eighteenth and nineteenth centuries, will not be discussed here. The term "renaissance" refers to the renewal of classical themes according to the level of scientific and artistic advancement from the thirteenth to the end of the sixteenth centuries. This classification is further subdivided into Early Renaissance, High Renaissance, and Late Renaissance. Little use is made of the term "Early Renaissance," although the works of Botticelli and Leonardo da Vinci would be late representatives of this category. The period is known for its emphasis on humanistic content presented in balanced, horizontal lines according to accepted principles of three-dimensional perspective. "High Renaissance" refers to the transitional period between 1500 and 1525, when Raffael and Michelangelo sought to deviate from the Early Renaissance traditions. The principle of this deviation was to create the masterpieces according to the concept of the artist instead of trying to mold art works according to the physical laws of perspective. This transition is detailed in Chapter II. The Late Renaissance carries forward the ideas of Michelangelo and Raffael, and is assigned a period from 1525 to 1590. The period is characterized by Mannerism, which varied from imitations of the Raffael style to surprising use of arrangement and color bearing little relation to the perceived nature of things, and by the rise of the Venetian school of artists: Titian, Paolo Veronese, and Tintoretto.

Roughly, these periods also correspond to developments in stage decoration. Leonardo da Vinci himself was also a late representative of Early Renaissance stage designing at the court in Milan. To

---

[1] "Baroque" is better described than defined. The word is of unknown origin, although perhaps related to *barroco,* a French word found also in Portuguese and meaning "rough pearl." As first used in reference to art, the term signified "irregularly shaped." The periodization of art styles in this section is derived from treatments found in the following sources: *Larousse Encyclopedia of Renaissance and Baroque Art,* general ed. René Huyghe (New York: Prometheus Press, 1964); Giorgio Castelfranco, *Leonardo da Vinci,* (New York: Harry N. Abrams, Inc., 1960); Benedetto Croce, *Aesthetic* (New York: The Noonday Press, 1960); Willi Flemming, *Deutsche Kultur im Zeitalter des Barock* (Potsdam: Akademische Verlagsgesellschaft Athenaion, 1931); Frederick Hartt, *Sandro Botticelli* (New York: Harry N. Abrams, Inc., 1953); Arnold Hauser, *Mannerism,* vols. 1 - 3 (London: Routledge and Kegan Paul, 1965); Eric New-ton, *European Painting and Sculpture* (Baltimore, Maryland: Penguin Books, 1962); Rudolf Stamm, ed., *Die Kunstformen des Barockzeitalters* (Bern: Francke Verlag, Sammlung Dalp, 1956); Wylie Sypher, *Four Stages of Renaissance Style* (Garden City, New York: Doubleday and Co., Inc., 1956); Victor Lucien Tapié, *The Age of Grandeur,* trans. from *Baroque et Classicisme* by A. Ross Williamson (New York: Grove Press, 1960); Hans Tintelnot, *Barocktheater und Barocke Kunst* (Berlin: Verlag Gerb. Mann, 1939): Werner Weisbach, *Der Barock als Kunst der Gegenreformation* (Berlin: P. Cassirer, 1921); Charles Wentinck, *El Greco* (New York: Barnes and Noble, Inc., 1964); Heinrich Woelfflin, *Renaissance and Baroque,* trans. Kathrin Simon (New York: Cornell University Press, 1966); Paul Zucker, *Styles in Painting* (New York: Viking Press, 1950) 4, 301 - 302.

the High Renaissance belongs the work of Raffael; and to the Late Renaissance, the work of Serlio.

In like manner and with like use of proper nouns, the age of baroque art is subdivided into Early Baroque, High Baroque, and Late Baroque. While baroque style is better described than defined, Early Baroque staging rises with the architecture of Aleotti at the Teatro Farnese (Parma, 1618-1619) and the flat wing scenery of Parigi. It extends to the mid-century *changement à vue* technology of Giacomo Torelli. The period roughly corresponds to the artistic achievements of El Greco. High Baroque art, then, extends from the mid-seventeenth century to the early part of the eighteenth century, and is characterized by the synthesis of previous tendencies by Ludovico Burnacini. The works of Ferdinando and Giuseppe Galli-Bibiena are Late Baroque creations. The historical stages of development employed by Allardyce Nicoll, John McDowell, and George Kernodle are acknowledged to be different from the ones used here. The eras of *cultural history* (not fine arts only) which have been used here are based on the well-established concepts employed by the leading German scholars: Heinz Kindermann, Hans Tintelnot, Willi Flemming, and Horst Richter.

Source Literature on High Baroque Culture

Current literature on the history of European baroque performances is being compiled mostly by German and Italian authors, as the bibliography shows. Of considerable help has been the *Theatergeschichte Europas,*[2] especially volume III, by Heinz Kindermann. This work is quite valuable for its large coverage and extensive bibliography of theatre history. Volume III, which deals with the history of the theatre during the baroque period, begins with a challenging analysis of baroque culture in relationship to theatre production. Since Kindermann has attempted to deal directly with drama and theatre materials, his history does not establish the relationships of theatre activity to evolving economic and historical patterns of Western culture. The mass of information covered has also precluded involvement in detailed treatment of special problems, although the conclusions presented in the text are amply supported by references to original materials in the appended footnotes and bibliography. In brief, the work of Kindermann is a rich source of data and ideas for continuing the development of research in theatre history.

A second general work of value has been that of Willi Flemming, *Deutsche Kultur im Zeitalter des Barock,* 1931.[3] This study has sought to present a topical analysis of various related trends current in the baroque era, including society, education, economics, art, philosophy, and theatre. Again, while the work lacks the precision for a detailed analysis of any special theme under these general headings, it is a monumental contribution to understanding the relationship of theatre activity to other facets of baroque culture in the German states.

Chapter III is greatly indebted to the careful monograph of Franz Hadamowsky on *Barocktheater am Wiener Kaiserhof,*[4] 1955. While not intending to discuss problems of theatre production, Hadamowsky has presented a fine, well documented description of the development and unity of dramatic performances at the Imperial Court from 1600 to 1750. Especially helpful is his detailed chronology of shows, together with the production artists and places of performance.

---

[2] Heinz Kindermann, *Theatergeschichte Europas,* Bd. III, IV (Salzburg: Otto Müller Verlag, 1959).

[3] Willi Flemming, *Deutsche Kultur im Zeitalter des Barock* (Potsdam, Germany: Akademische Verlagsgesellschaft Athenaion, 1931).

[4] Franz Hadamowsky, *Barocktheater am Wiener Kaiserhof* (Wien: Verlag A. Sexl, 1955).

The most important initial research on Giovanni and Ludovico Burnacini was published by Flora Biach-Schiffmann in 1931 and is available on film number 123 at The Ohio State University Theatre Collection.[5] As indicated and will be noted again later, the original biographical material and classification of the Burnacini material by Biach-Schiffmann is now out of date, as regards accuracy of early activity and comprehensiveness of pictorial data. Flora Biach-Schiffmann did not intend to accomplish more than a face validity description of the scenic materials she presented; consequently, the whole problem of purpose and function of designs in relation to actual production did not enter her treatment. In spite of limitations which commonly accrue to the aging of any research monograph, the work of Biach-Schiffmann is still the largest published record identifying and locating original Burnacini materials.

The major document in research on Ludovico Burnacini and his art is that of Guido Adler, *Il Pomo D'Oro*, which appeared in 1896 as Jahrg. III/2 - Bd.6 of *Denkmäler der Tonkunst in Österreich.*[6] The introduction, a conservative and scholarly statement of the history of the performance together with a description of the story and music, is followed by the complete libretto, music for Acts I, II, and IV, and twenty-four designs, which are discussed in Chapter 7 of the present study.

A most recent publication, on which much of the material in Chapter 8 is based, is the work of Horst Richter on Johann Oswald Harms, 1963.[7] This work enables one to acquire a better picture of the Burnacini influence in northern German states after 1679. The book presents a detailed biography of J. O. Harms, together with analyses of his ballet designs. These analyses are done with a view to actual production problems. In a concluding chapter, Richter has attempted an analysis of baroque scene designs by type, discussing the contributions of various artists to the different items in the typology. The present study will apply similar principles to the Cortina production of *Il pomo d'oro*.

Perhaps the two most outstanding works in English are those of George R. Kernodle, *From Art to Theatre,*[8] and Simon T. Worsthorne, *Venetian Opera in the Seventeenth Century.*[9] The research of George Kernodle, as the title *From Art to Theatre* suggests, is concerned with the derivation of renaissance and baroque staging technique from the *tableaux vivants,* small emblematic paintings used in medieval processions. The relationships and development of the *tableaux* in connection with the theatre is traced through the Rederyker stages of the Lowlands, the Elizabethan stages, the improvised marketplace stages on the mainland of the continent, the Teatro Olimpico, and the perspective scene of the baroque period. Throughout the work, Kernodle restates his thesis that in modern times art precedes stage décor; that the principles of illusion and of symbolism were laid before the renaissance theatre architects were born. Therefore, one understands renaissance staging only through a study of the aesthetic forms in paintings handed down to the scene designers. The thesis of Kernodle is a formidable one, so long as one does not question two assumptions: 1. That the anonymous painters of the *tableaux vivants* used none of the tiny theatre-like models which artists have sometimes employed to assist themselves in developing aesthetic perspective;   2. That the *tableaux vivants* painters were isolated specialists, generating their concepts *a priori,* in an age when virtually all other art-

[5] Flora Biach-Schiffmann, *Giovanni und Ludovico Burnacini, Theater und Feste am Wiener Hofe* (Wien-Berlin: Krystall-Verlag, 1931); OSUTC 123.

[6] Guido Adler, *Denkmäler der Tonkunst in Österreich,* Jahrg. III/2 - Bd. 6; Marc Antonio Cesti, *Il Pomo D'Oro* (Graz: Akademische Druck- und Verlagsanstalt, 1896, 1959).

[7] Horst Richter, *Johann Oswald Harms,* Ein deutscher Theater-

dekorateur des Barock (Emsdetten(Westf.): Verlag Lechte, 1963).

[8] George R. Kernodle, *From Art to Theatre* (Chicago: The University of Chicago Press, 1947).

[9] Simon T. Worsthorne, *Venetian Opera in the Seventeenth Century* (Oxford: Clarendon Press, 1954).

ists were generally educated in a wide variety of skills, many of which could be readily employed in the theatre. Were not research materials of theatre history much more ephemeral than those in the plastic arts, one might reasonably hope that some day evidence would be found to show that designers of perspective scenes existed before the painters of the *tableaux vivants* were born.

Venetian Opera by Simon T. Worsthorne presents excellent historical background, technical design and stage information, together with a detailed treatment of elements basic to early opera: spectacle, aria, chorus, and orchestra. A concluding section relates Venetian opera to the aesthetics of the seventeenth century with its interest in realism, manners, and fantasy. The particular difficulty with both books mentioned is that neither author could rightly extend his research to the events in Vienna during the seventeenth century. Some effort has been spent recently in presenting the fine accomplishments of the Galli-Bibiena family to researchers in English speaking countries, but the Bibienas belong to baroque culture in its later, triumphant period, not to the art of the Early and High Baroque periods. Since the purpose of the Mayor study[10] seems, furthermore, to have been biographical in nature with supporting illustrations of designing potential, the theatrical functions of the Bibiena iconographs remain quite obscure, except as they may correlate with the earlier work of Joseph Gregor in Vienna and with the recent Juvarra research at The Ohio State University Theatre Collection, reported in *The Ohio State University Theatre Collection Bulletin for 1964.*[11] In that research, John Bielenberg, using original evidence of the Juvarra designs and three-dimensional illustrations based on a model of his own making for the reconstruction of Juvarra settings, was able to demonstrate the feasibility of an axial perspective technique common to the Galli-Bibienas through the use of cut-out, profile wing units. These wings could be deployed most anywhere on the stage and even turned at oblique and right angles to the front of the stage if so desired.

Among the publications in English, a noteworthy contribution to the understanding of High Baroque performances is the Patricia Kean translation of *Essays on Opera*[12] by Egon Wellesz. This series of essays, which is similar in methodology to the plan adopted here, is primarily concerned with early opera as a vehicle for the development of musical forms. In order to demonstrate the relationship between action and musical innovations, Egon Wellesz has devoted an entire chapter to the descriptive analysis of *Il pomo d'oro.* In many respects, his descriptive analysis correlates well with the findings to be presented in our Chapter 7. But the limitations of Wellesz in problems of stage decoration become rather evident from statements such as the following: "Yet the work of the composer . . . was the centre of interest and while poetry and stage architecture did not undergo any real development . . ."[13] "Act I . . . The hall of pillars remains the same. Only the ornaments are changed . . . In the clouds Pegasus is replaced by a dragon breathing fire with Discord, . . ."[14] "Now the clouds sink down and conceal the assembly of the Gods."[15] In view of the materials now available, the explanations to be presented in Chapter 7 will be markedly different from those just quoted.

Other than the sources given, literature in English on baroque theatrical performances is sparse. While James Laver has expressed interest for Continental theatre of this era, his emphasis on the cos-

---

[10] A. Hyatt Mayor, *The Bibiena Family* (New York: H. Bittner and Co., 1945); Giuseppe Galli-Bibiena, *Architectural and Perspective Designs,* introduction by A. Hyatt Mayor (New York: Dover Publications, 1964); *Monumenta Scenica,* introduction by Joseph Gregor (Berkeley, California: Samuel J. Hume, Inc., 1954).

[11] John Bielenberg, "A Three-Dimensional Study of Two Scene Designs by Fillippo Juvarra" in *The Ohio State University Theatre Collection Bulletin,* No. 11 (Columbus, Ohio: The Ohio State University, 1964).

[12] Egon Wellesz, *Essays on Opera,* trans. Patricia Kean (New York: Roy Publishers, 1950).

[13] *Ibid.,* 57.

[14] *Ibid.,* 63.

[15] *Ibid.,* 67.

tume and décor of drama has been attended at times by inaccuracies concerning other matters in theatre history.[16] *Drama Its Costume and Décor* is a very readable history of costuming and stage designs.
In it, much reliance is placed upon highly qualified, reputable secondary sources: Joseph Gregor,
Margarete Bieber, George Kernodle, and Allardyce Nicoll. To this extent, the book also has its limitations. James Laver quite candidly admits his concern for the implementation of available knowledge,
rather than for the accumulation of new and undigested data devoted to the critical evaluation of current hypotheses. His history brings much worthwhile, illustrative material relating to the implementation of masks, costumes, and techniques in performances during the different ages of the theatre in
Western culture. The chapter on "The Expansion of the Baroque" contributes excellent examples of
baroque staging techniques. In two paragraphs on Ludovico Burnacini, however, Laver asserts that
the architect was born in Vienna and that he collaborated with Torelli on the production of *La Finta
Pazza* at Venice. From the evidence accumulated in Chapter 6, both assertions of James Laver seem
highly improbable. A further limitation of *Drama Its Costume and Décor,* pertaining to the problem
and objectives of this study, is that James Laver does not purport to discuss the means by which identifiable iconographic materials were realized in the process of actual stage production.

Allardyce Nicoll traces the development of theatrical places and performances after the medieval
period through Italy, France, and England.[17] For these movements, Nicoll has supplied a large resource
of material which has contributed significantly to the comprehension of theatre history. The absence
of detailed discussion on other European trends in the history of the theatre is not easily accounted for,
although linguistic barriers probably proved insurmountable in most cases. In an appendix, he does
present a well known print of the Cortina Theatre, illustrating the opening performance of *Il pomo
d'oro;* but the picture date differs considerably from the date most commonly assigned to it.

Baroque and Romantic Stage Design, which János Scholz published in 1950,[18] is useful for orientation to general trends in designing, but it is of little help for interpreting the Viennese designs of
the seventeenth century since no production purpose is stated for the scenes presented. While the study
is valuable for identifying iconographic materials of the period described, it lacks a functional analysis such as proved helpful to the Bielenberg research on the Juvarra designs.

Purpose of the Research

The purpose of this study is as follows: (1) to indicate the nature and manner of theatrical performances at the Imperial Court under the leadership of the Burnacinis; (2) to demonstrate the appli-
cation of High Baroque concepts in the production of *Il pomo d'oro;* (3) to suggest the probable significance of baroque theatre at Vienna for the history of theatre throughout Central Europe, and (4)
to help fill a gap in theatre history written in English. Unquestionably, one of the most significant features of baroque festive performances at the Imperial Court was the pre-eminent educational significance which the Habsburg family assigned to the theatre for the political and cultural unification of
the Holy Roman Empire.

---

[16] James Laver, *Drama Its Costume and Décor* (London: The Studio Publications, 1951), 110-145; Ludovico Burnacini was
only five years old when Torelli created the designs for the production of *La Finta Pazza* in Venice.

[17] Allardyce Nicoll, *The Development of the Theatre* (London:

Harrap and Co., Ltd., 1958). On the basis of data supplied by
Franz Hadamowsky, the date which is assumed here for the
opening performance of *Il pomo d'oro* is 1668.

[18] János Scholz, *Baroque and Romantic Stage Design* (New York:
Beechhurst Press, 1950).

The main justification of the present inquiry is much more than the translation into English of a sizeable amount of research literature which now exists chiefly in German works on the topic. A critical difference of method and procedure exists in the treatment of original materials. Pursuing his inquiry on "A Three-Dimensional Study of Two Scene Designs by Filippo Juvarra," John Bielenberg noted that,

> Hundreds of designs have been preserved and have been admired for their theatrical use of perspective, but the lack of accompanying floor plans or working drawings stymies the research- er in his attempt to determine just how the design was actually realized on stage in tradition- al wing and shutter units.[19]

It is precisely this last note, "to determine just how the design was actually realized on stage . . .," which is intended to distinguish this research from the vast amount of literature already existing. Bar- ring a momentous discovery of new material, however, the work here undertaken labors under the difficulties of having no floor plans, not even sketched ones, and no working drawings. For the most part, only metal etchings of L. O. Burnacini's productions have been preserved, and the limitations of such idealized representations in theatre history is so well known as hardly to require further dem- onstration here. Nevertheless, as pointed out by Franz Hadamowsky, while one may expect that the engraved scenes might be somewhat grander than the reality presented on the stage, the artists leave us amazed by their aesthetic talent, their technical means, and their industry unfolded in the theatres.[20] Yet, if one accepts the limitations inherent to any treatment of these designs, the proper use of valid methodology may still permit of some reasonable conjectures.

Methodology

The procedure which has been selected, therefore, is that which has been employed and frequent- ly found to be fruitful at The Ohio State University Theatre Collection. With the objective of provid- ing a "reconstruction of theatre history," the Theatre Collection at The Ohio State University has sought to include all valuable clues obtainable from original "scripts, prompt books, scene and costume de- signs, technical treatises, posters, programs, and reviews."[21]

A second feature of the procedure is the cataloging of the materials acquired. First, each item is classified chronologically, according to a historical period. Twelve ages of the theatre have been assigned; e.g., a *Hamlet* design by Gordon Craig is cataloged under scene design of the early twen- tieth century.

Second, "Each item is classified according to genre,"[22] seven major categories being employed: artist, costume, lighting, scene design, staging, play script, and theatre architecture. Subdivisions are used to make the classification more comprehensive.

Third, "Each item is classified according to its medium,"[23] such as legitimate theatre, cinema, television, etc.

Fourth, the classification makes use of "national origins." Wherever possible, subdivisions are employed to help students in research on staging trends of England, Germany, Italy, Belgium, etc.

---

[19] John E. Bielenberg, *op. cit.,* no. 11, 6.
[20] Franz Hadamowsky, *op. cit.,* 6, 51-56.
[21] John C. Morrow, "O.S.U. Theatre Collection: A Unique Facility,"

Players Magazine, Vol. XLI, No. 2, November, 1964, 57-58.
[22] *Ibid.*
[23] *Ibid.*

In order that the classification may be as complete as possible, the seven major theatre categories are cross-indexed.

In reconstructing the history of the theatre for courses and research studies, the foregoing system of classification is utilized to help create a historico-cultural setting for an understanding of the period and works to be considered. Then, by utilizing material classified under national origins, one can proceed to analyse, for example, different theatrical movements both within and outside England during the Elizabethan Age. In contrast to many theatre histories, which identify materials but lack a functional classification for understanding production problems, the method of functional analysis and reconstruction adopted at The Ohio State University Theatre Collection is intended to reduce some of the guessing involved with the usual handling of theatre materials by the addition of two steps, prior to a final synthesis of information:

1. Factors and facets of theatrical activity are selected and demonstrated analytically for their cognate relationships within the period under consideration.
2. The material is arranged for a detailed comprehension of audience, production, and performance relationships. This step commonly entails the analysis and demonstration of pictorial evidence, sequentially arranged.

The final synthesis accomplished by the functional method described is often best achieved through the consideration of some singularly outstanding performance which most typifies and fittingly illustrates the period under discussion. Within the limits of this study such a treatment is accorded the opera, *Il pomo d'oro.*

Conclusion

In view of the purpose, materials, and methodology which have been discussed, the results anticipated may be stated as follows:

1. The significance of Ludovico O. Burnacini as the leader of the post-Torelli generation in Continental designing.
2. The detailing of aesthetic elements peculiar to baroque staging and theatrical performances.
3. The applicability of these elements in the production of *Il pomo d'oro.*
4. The addition of primary materials associated with the Viennese baroque influence into English literature on the history of theatre.
5. The influence of the *Theater auf der Cortina* and related places of performance on subsequent architectural and scenic effects in Central Europe.

Other results may be expected to indicate the relationship and implications of Viennese Court performances for political education in the Holy Roman Empire. To the extent that the aforementioned results are successfully demonstrated, they may be taken severally or in sum-total as further confirmation of the critical methodology employed at The Ohio State University Theatre Collection.

Illustrations, maps, and designs relevant to successive issues as they arise will be arranged to accompany the chapter discussions of those issues in the main body of the text.

Part I:
Viennese Culture in Transition

Economics, Society,

and *Virtus Heroica*

1

The Transition in Economics

The period of High Baroque culture finds its centers in the states of southern Germany, and chiefly in Vienna, which came to be the capital of The Holy Roman Empire under the Habsburg dynasty. The characteristics of this period imply a continuity of many developments in art, music, and theatre which have already been mentioned. But often the transition to High Baroque culture is a strengthening of previous influences attended by peculiar innovations of its own. In the history of theatre, this period, covering the second half of the seventeenth century, is called the post-Torelli generation, although Torelli remained a dominant figure for almost two decades of it. Nevertheless, the most important rising star of this generation, and the person whose work must receive the greatest share of attention later, was Ludovico O. Burnacini.

The shift of baroque culture from Venice and Spain to the southern German states was not without practical considerations. The Thirty Years' War which ended with The Peace of Westphalia in 1648 had desolated the German Hanseatic towns to the North, had broken the power of The Hanseatic League, and had served as a temporary setback to the Dutch economy in the Lowlands. Trade moved southward. Leipzig displaced Lübeck as a fur market.[1] Cologne broke away from the League in an effort to monopolize English trade on the Continent. To avoid the vicissitudes of fortune which alternately placed Venice at the mercy of the French and the Turks, new inland centers of wealth grew in Dresden, Vienna and Munich. The Habsburgs also had at their disposal rich metal and gold mines in Hungary.

---

[1] Herbert Heaton, *Economic History of Europe* (New York: Harper & Brothers, 1948), 259.

In the closing decades of the seventeenth century, two former Hanseatic towns, Lübeck and Hamburg, were to experience economic revival under the leadership of the Hohenzollern family at the more secure inland towns of Hanover and Brunswick.[2] At this time, France, hemmed in on three sides by "The Grand Alliance" of the Lutheran Hohenzollern nobility, the Jesuit stronghold of Emperor Leopold I, and the victorious commercial classes of England with their Lowland King, William of Orange, fell into decline. In place of Louis XIV, Leopold I became the dominant voice on the Continent.

Correlative with the rise of new power centers was the rise of cultural influence. Contemporaneously with the cultural influence originating at Vienna, Henry Purcell was developing masque themes into an independently composed libretto for *Dido and Aeneas* in London about 1683. Other favorites for music and scenic display were *The Prophetess, King Arthur,* and *The Fairy Queen.* But an early death at thirty-six terminated the brief fame of Purcell. Dryden had also composed a libretto for *Albion and Albanius,* performed at the Queen's Theatre in Dorset Garden in 1691. But native British contribution to opera in the High Baroque period virtually ended with these few works. During the first few decades of the following century, operas again became fashionable in London, but with librettos done in Italian rather than in English.[3]

The rising Prussian nobility sponsored numerous ballets, operas, and large theatre constructions at Dresden, Brunswick, Hanover, and Hamburg; but the strongest impulse for cultural leadership seemed to center at Vienna.

Transition in Social Organization

In the matter of social organization, rank and personal will decided the precise order and membership in any group. The fairly well understood distinctions of social order and membership offered a firm basis for the structure of social life. The distinctions are well indicated in the illustration of the *Theater auf der Cortina* (Figure 1), representing the opening performance of *Il pomo d'oro.* The auditorium, which was the most significant new construction of the German baroque art, conveys the most fitting picture for the social stratification of the epoch. It is a gallery theatre, the Viennese Imperial Court Theatre. The emperor, Leopold I, in the best seat—"the duke's seat"—opposite the stage scene, surrounded by his court—these constitute the first and honored gallery. The second gallery brings together the high officialdom, the servants of Leopold's absolute state. In the third gallery are seated the honorable citizenry, business people and tradesmen whose greater pride it is to bear a title of Court Supplier, or Master Duster of the court chambers. The fourth gallery, near the ceiling could be used to accommodate the lower ranks of servants; not only of the Court, but of the aristocracy and upper classes generally. On the ground floor, at the rear and sides of the auditorium, hungry masses could be allowed to stream in who had no legitimate connection with, or obligation to, the Imperial Court.[4] If admitted, the masses would at most be endured by the higher social orders and often be referred to with some undignified epithet as Pöbel or Pöfel.[5] Such people, who had been the well-springs of

[2] *Ibid.,* 260.

[3] Eric Walter White, *The Rise of English Opera* (New York: The Philosophical Library, 1951), 38-46, 49. The date for the *Dido* production varies between 1683-1689. The exact date is not of material importance to the conclusions reached here.

[4] Willi Flemming, *op. cit.,* 29-30.

[5] cf. the current slang term "crud" used in the United States to designate any person or group considered to be very low class in social behavior. N.B., The Cortina illustration offered by Flemming has been misdated 1688, instead of 1668. A. Nicoll further misdated the scene as 1686 instead of 1668. The scene design was included with the first published text of *Il pomo d'oro.*

Figure 1.   Ludovico Burnacini, *Theater auf der Cortina, Il pomo d'oro,* 1668

inspiration for the new art of opera, were really down deep in the social order; and they were likewise deep in the Parterre entrance ways. They were not on an eye level with the stage; but had to look up to the elegant performances, and look high with envy to the glamorous ladies and gentlemen in the galleries. Court guards with spears kept a careful view on the actions and behavior of the mob, for they were sometimes known to be a very disturbing and intolerable little group of people.

The Transition in Human Ideals

Given the conditions stated, what may be said further as to the cultural specifics and the human ideals cultivated in the southern German baroque society? Willi Flemming preferred to rank the new sense of elevated self-importance as the distinquishing mark of German baroque culture. A portrait of Frans Hals, he observes, looks directly at the viewer and announces, "Have a look at what I am!"[6] While baroque man thus accentuates his self-importance, his portrait painters further idealize the egos of their subjects. The baroque man so idealized is not calm, but he does show an overwhelming sense of self-esteem. His attitude is less conditioned from within, however, than it receives support and strength from idealized, religious sources depicted as being above the person and his experience.

[6] Willi Flemming, *op. cit.,* 3-17.

Figure 2.   Design by J. W. Baumgarten. The unfolding of pomp and glory for heightening religious feeling. From W. Flemming, *Deutsche Kultur im Zeitalter des Barock.*

Yet Baroque-man is not subjectivistic in his own self-image. With all of his self-righteous feeling and conduct, he does not conceive his ego as the only existence and value in the world. There is a polar opposite, a higher power to be experienced, one which seems to draw him beyond himself into a higher communion (Figure 2). It is from this higher communion that his ego receives its sense of elevated power, acquires its certitude, and receives its potential to affirm an independent existence and to make its claims valid. But the worlds remain distinct; the finite, enclosed world of soulish man is confronted with the sphere of the Spirit-God, whose existence is also objective and absolutely valid. The latter commands complete obedience; man can do no more than obey the incomprehensible will of the Divine. Such is the ethico-religious attitude of the human ideal in the baroque era.

What frequently seems pompous to people in the twentieth century may well have been the result of a baroque person's insatiable drive of curiosity. Whether angels and saints, as in the churches, or a multitude of love affairs, baroque man is a collector of curiosities. Given the necessary wealth, everything lovely, new, or fashionable is admissable.[7] The baroque man collects all sorts of art objects and curiosities for which he has gladly travelled far. By extensive correspondence he cultivates close social ties. The printing press receives wide attention for purposes of publishing enormous editions of collected writings and for establishing newspapers with which to feed the ravenous curiosity seekers. Rapid conquest of foreign markets; quick imitation of the fashionable—these are not merely the danger, but the leading characteristic of the time.

Educationally, the chief weight of emphasis during the baroque period fell on the training of the memory. The new national school movements, including those of such reformers as Ratke and Comenius, spent considerable time on memorization. Cultural leaders often embellished their lives with a vast array of skills and hundreds of little information bits which did not always suggest a sense of unity and purpose. Pansophism, universal knowledge of all real existence, was the affirmed goal of Comenius's core curriculum theories. Extensive footnotes became the fashion for programs supplied the audiences at the theatres.[8] The mastery of rhetorical commonplaces and literary excerpts flourished. For stage production, one needed a memory filled with technical rules and examples from recognized classics, an appreciation of Ciceronian style and language, and a flair for highly decorative embellishment. The cultivation of the memory was also a fundamental principle for good manners.

Once again, a particularly striking characteristic of baroque culture was its sense-realism (Figure 3). Whether it be the pansophism of Comenius, the prose and poetry of John Milton, the theories of John Locke, or the baroque culture and drama of the Jesuits on the Continent, a first appeal was made to the sense impressions, which were associated in some massive unity by means of the sense-organs. Nevertheless, the baroque approach to art is not identical with early twentieth century naturalism. In the midst of the multitude of sense appeals a principle of selectivity is highly operative. All selected impressions are constantly related to the ego motif. In the case of the numerous hues which were introduced, an interesting manner of shading occurs—with red perhaps also a rose, blood-red, coral, or purple—as well as a sensitivity for strongly contrasting light and dark.

The tendency to disregard limits, but with heightened contrast, makes the appeal to sense-realism most striking. The baroque character is determined to produce an effect, to make an impression, to have resonance; it awaits an audience applause. It seems to be always on-stage, exciting public responses.[9] In some of the arts, this seeming arrogance is an important motivating power, extending

[7] *Ibid.*, 9.
[8] *Ibid.*, 13-14.
[9] *Ibid.*, 15.

Figure 3.   Disturbing, macabre representation with intentional sense-realism. *The Damnation* by Balthaser Permoser. W. Flemming, *op. cit.*

Figure 4.   Ideal man of the Baroque: strong-willed, lordly nature. A bust of Anton Ulrich von Braunschweig by Balthaser Permoser.
W. Flemming, *op. cit.*

to organ contests among leading musicians. Applause is sought in order to strengthen the ego, so that the hero may drink deeply from his draughts of success. With this attitude is also the danger of inflated pomposity, posing, grand declamation, empty phrase and pomp. These are the darker sides of baroque culture. But the highest achievement is also true flights of the imagination, genuine pathos, and structures of monumental worth. These results are the product of passionate, but completely personal commitments to the ideal of the Absolute.

In consideration of the foregoing observations on German baroque culture—its elevated self-importance, its reverence for ethical and religious absolutes objectively beyond the individual, its ravenous curiosity for the novel and the antiquarian collections, its training of the memory, its sense-realism, and its desire for extremes which will evoke public applause—one gains insight and understanding for the baroque's ideal man. His structure and bent is heroic. The age itself chose a term to express its own spiritual bent, "courageous."[10] A tragedy by Gryphius bore the title "The Courageous Law Student, or dying Aemilius Paulus Papinianus." Lohenstein also gave his fictional heroes the special designation of "courageous Commander Arminius." Even the authors of Latin texts on ethics discovered that the highest virtue worthy of the title *virtus heroica* was that which grew out of courage and magnanimity. The illustrated bust of Anton Ulrich von Braunschweig (Figure 4), nobleman and leader of baroque theatrical performances in northern Germany during the last two decades of the seventeenth century, demonstrates the ideal. Here one sees a strength of soul, with passions and drives so well disciplined and subordinated as to serve the ethical ego. This moral ego seems thereby capable of acting with a free and determined will which is in proportion to the demands of its cultural ethos. In a later age, Goethe could form his *Faust* for a world journey, and his *Egmont,* by comparison, could show the historical development of a youthful, fiery romantic; similarly, Schiller develops *Maria Stuart.* But Gryphius in the baroque era presents his *Catherine of Georgia* in the Scottish queen's actual age, developing his strongest character accents from motherly feelings and widowhood. The chief concern seems to be with the establishment of a firm ego, certainly not with development and maturity.[11]

Yet, once again, the baroque magnanimity receives its high inspiration through a sense of personal communion with a divine power which reaches beyond the individual. This sense of communion is expressed in the completely personal consciousness that the individual is borne on the everlasting arms of an eternal Redeemer. Theology of the time did tend to be expressed in dramatic metaphors. Magnanimity was no final assurance of life beyond the grave, but it helped overcome the fears of death and seemed to earn its possessor genuine fame and the highest honor. Public applause would come to a man of honor; he was certain of it, and he expected to hear it. The applause was his stimulus to perseverance, and the voice of the crowd was his confirmation that he had acted rightly.[12]

[10] *Ibid.,* 15.
[11] *Ibid.,* 16.
[12] *Ibid.,* 17.

2

Baroque Art Forms in Austria

The Transition in Plastic Art

If the chief characteristics of the High Renaissance are taken to be those best expressed in the works of such representatives as Botticelli, Leonardo da Vinci, and Piero della Francesca, then certain notable emphases become clear.[1] Comparing Figures 5 to 9, one can observe that all of these artists have emphasized human qualities in their compositions. The biblical and mythological elements are embellishments of the fundamentally natural settings and human materials. Renaissance Man as the measurer of all things appears strong, self-assured, happy, and intelligent, able to assimilate into himself the whole of classical culture.[2] Predominant in the era are the artistic concepts of proportion, harmony, clarity, and a comprehensive unity in diversity. Throughout the art creations of the period, the same emphasis falls on the adoption of a scenic vanishing point, the development of illusionary perspective, and the primacy of horizontal lines by which each artist gives a humanistic, this-worldly, and naturalistic resolution to the problem of space. In contrast to courtly armored knights and meditating saints which dominated artistic ideals during the Middle Ages, the renaissance artist makes the rational and happy man the handsome hero of the ancients. One may note further that the heavenly properties of Leonardo's angel are less indicative of other-worldly interests than they are of anatomy, aeronautics, and engineering.

[1] F. Hartt, *Sandro Botticelli* (New York: Pocket Books, Inc., 1953); G. Castelfranco, *Leonardo Da Vinci* (New York: Pocket Books, Inc., 1960).

[2] Paul H. Lang, *Music in Western Civilization* (New York: W. W. Norton and Company, Inc., 1941), 321-324.

Figure 6. Piero della Francesca: national setting and town setting useful for a comedy. Emphasis is on the use of horizontal lines in geometrical perspective with vanishing points to infinity. L. Simonson, *The Art of Scenic Design.*

Baroque art finds its strongest origins with an artist who has sometimes been considered the giant of the High Renaissance, Michelangelo. He, more than any other, states Lang, threw all the aforementioned interests "overboard."[3] Once again vertical dimensions vie with horizontal motifs and curving, muscular corporeality for a new harmonic unison. The unity is not achieved. The result continues to be a humanistic concern, but with a shift of mood from human drama to human tragedy. As described by Paul Lang, Michelangelo's figures seem to writhe, groan, and sigh under the burden of massive corporeality which makes them even more the prisoners of material, sensuous space than is the case with ordinary mortals.[4] With the innovations of Michelangelo, shown in Figure 10, the problem of aesthetic space seems farther from resolution than ever before. The task of achieving a new synthesis was the work which confronted the artists of the baroque era.

The Venetian schools of Titian, Jacopo Robusti (called Tintoretto because his father was a dyer), and Paolo Veronese contributed much to the development of decentralization, of illusionary movement,

[3] *Ibid.*

Figure 5. Botticelli, "Minerva Punishes the Centaur": a mythical embellishment of human figures, using natural setting in perspective with emphasis on horizontal dimensions proceeding to a vanishing point above the mountain top in the distance.

Figure 7.   Botticelli, *The Birth of Venus,* Uffizi, Florence, c. 1488. The rolling sea, supporting shell which appears to move amid the waves, flying zephyrs, and forest wings were all common to renaissance staging as described by Sabbatine and Furttenbach. One of the hours is about to clothe Venus in a robe.

Figure 8.   Botticelli, *The Miracles of Saint Zenobius,* c. 1500. The Medieval multiple setting with its asymmetrical, balanced perspective, was entirely possible to realize on a stage equipped with Serlian wings. Windows painted on Serlian wings might well be black as a result of perspective staging practices.

Figure 9. Leonardo da Vinci: "The Annunciation." Emphasis again is on horizontal lines proceeding into the infinite distance. The angel is a strong, self-assured, happy, intelligent renaissance man, employed by the artist for additional speculations on anatomy and engineering.

Figure 10.   Michelangelo (1475-1564), *The Persian Sibyl.* The horizontal dimensions have been moved aside to create room for more vertical dimensions distorted by large curves and muscular corporeality. The same motif is carried to the smaller figures at either side. Decentralization was a leading characteristic of Mannerism.

and of new hues, the first two of which are shown in Figure 11. But, the most creative synthesis of all previous concepts which possessed a convincing emotional unity, drawn from a unique combination of line, color, light, and shadow, was the achievement of Domenikos Theotokopoulos, known better as El Greco. His productions may very well be considered the embodiment of baroque Spain. Once again the transcendental penchant for vertical dimensions is predominant. As the religious and metaphysical motifs occupy the upper center of the composition, some elements of this world look on with profound solemnity while others turn their eyes upward in ecstacy (Figure 12). Serpentine-like lines and greatly distorted anatomical features draped in massive, flowing garments create a setting of unrest and tension yearning for religious peace, symbolized in the display of light. And it is El Greco who dominates the new ideals of baroque art. The concordance of proportions for its own sake is no longer of interest; the new spirit likes the vertical dimension, arbitrary disproportion, and excessive measures aimed at a new religious synthesis (Figures 13 - 15A and B).

[4]*Ibid.,* 322.

Figure 11.   Venetian Painting in the Sixteenth Century: Top left: Titian, *The Entombment.* Bottom left: Tintoretto, *The Last Supper.* Right: Paolo Veronese, *The Apotheosis of Venice.* E. Newton, *op. cit.*

Figure 12.   El Greco, *Worship of the Shepherds* (Prado, Madrid). The bulging distortions of earlier painters are radically distorted to achieve a new synthesis of line, color, and light contrast. Building arches are made higher to give a new resolution to problems of space. The vanishing point is also moved to the top-center. Vertical dimensions are predominant. Illusionary movement is turbulently dynamic.

Figure 13.   El Greco, *Assumption of the Virgin Mary* (Museo de San Vicente, Toledo). Baroque art developed the innovations of line, illusionary movement, light and color contrasts given by Mannerists into a dynamic synthesis of setting and movement by resolving spatial conflicts.

Figure 14.   El Greco, *Mount Sinai* (c. 1570, authenticity uncertain; in Galleria Estence, Modena, Italy). The asymmetrical positioning of the mountains foreshadows the work of Juvarra and Oswald Harms in theatre designing after 1700. The lightning effect was already traditional in Late Renaissance staging. The mountain and stairway dimensions, however, are more similar to the modern designing of Gordon Craig.

Figure 15A. Jacopo della Quercia, *The Creation of Adam.* cf. figure 15B, Bernini's vision of St. Theresa for a recapitulation of differences between the horizontal symmetry of renaissance art and the more dynamic, vertical synthesis of baroque art, as demonstrated by sculpture. E. Newton, *op. cit.*

Figure 15B.

The Transition in Music

Michelangelo, the Venetian schools, and El Greco had equally bold colleagues among the musicians of the day. The return of Gothic strivings was not less characteristic of the musicians than it was of the creators in the fine arts. Signs of the new age were already evident in the boundless torrent of music noticed in Ockeghem's works. A stream of sonority, symbolizing the unutterable, appears in Venetian chording. An aging Palestrina uses mystical chords to reflect the spirit of the Counter Reformation.[5] Yet these great masters all remained within the limits of the *a cappella* style.

Baroque music may be considered to begin with the Venetian creations of Giovanni Gabrieli (1557 - 1612). Thus in music, as also in painting, — for El Greco had received his basic training in the Venetian schools — Venice was the leading center of early baroque culture. Using multiple choirs and a multitude of instruments to compose his orchestra, Gabrieli created elaborate tonal murals to express the monumental drama of the baroque age. When *ricercar* and *toccata* were evolved into instrumental-contrapuntal forms, having no connection with vocal models, the ground was prepared for the arrival of baroque culture's chief instrumental form, the fugue.[6] Another residue of the polychoral style was the development of instrumental ensembles, including organ ensembles rivaling each other in virtuosity.

The Transition in Theatre Staging

Likewise in the theatre new developments characterized the age of baroque art. Here also, the transition from renaissance art to baroque art was a transition in line emphasis, from the dominance of horizontal lines to the dominance of vertical dimensions. The illusionary perspective was retained. Every wing would still be related to a scenic vanishing point upstage, corresponding to an opposite point of distance, the *duke's seat* in the auditorium. The set would still create a sense of symmetrical balance and proportion, but with a much less raked stage. The decrease in the rake of the stage was made possible by the adoption of a wing and shutter system in place of the angle wings which characterized the Serlian stage of the Late Renaissance and Manneristic eras.

During the Early Baroque era, Aleotti and Parigi (cf. p. 23) had successfully executed a revolution in theatrical staging from realistic three-dimensional wings, as shown in the *periaktoi* illustrations (Figure 16), and the Serlian wings in the Street Scene from Piero della Francesca (Figure 6), to a painted perspective on two-dimensional wings (Figure 17). With painted perspective and increased depth, action could be permitted on the stage area within the wings, and the rake of the stage could be reduced, eventually to a height of 20 cm. for a 10m. deep stage at Herrenhausen Gardens, an outdoor theatre of Lower Saxony which was built in 1689.[7] The moving of the flat wings on and off stage was executed manually, with the wings themselves being set in grooves on the stage floor.

A further technical revolution in theatre construction and staging took place when Giacomo Torelli mechanized the wing and shutter scene changing, the *changement à vue,* by the introduction of

[5] *Ibid.,* 323.

[6] *Ibid.,* 324. *Ricercar:* the disguising of a theme by various contrapuntal alterations; *toccata:* a composition for a keyboard instrument; *fugue:* a polyphonic composition according to the laws of counterpoint.

[7] Dr. Rudolf Meyer, *Hecken- und Gartentheater* (Emsdetten, Germany: Verlag H. v. J. Lechte, 1934), 135 and Abb. 33.

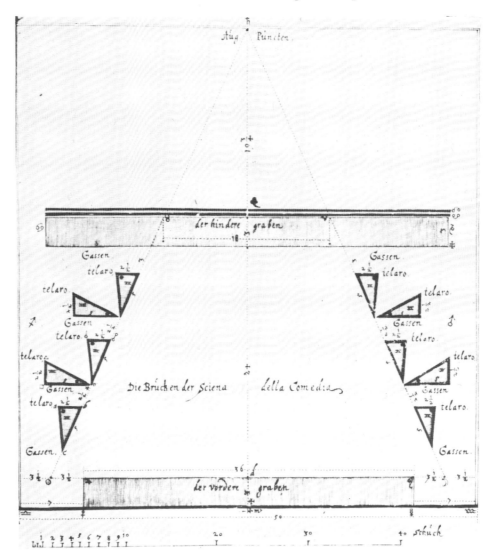

Ground Plan of the Setting

Scene Shifting with Periaktoi

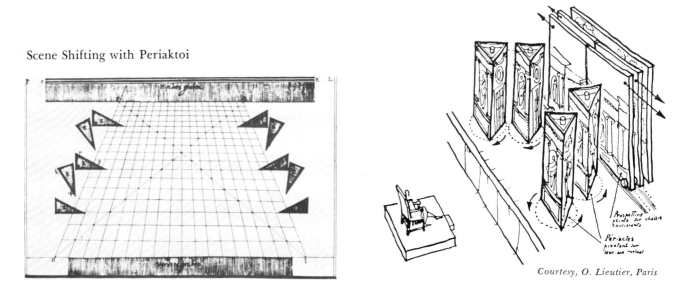

Courtesy, O. Lieutier, Paris

Figure 16.   A Manneristic design of J. Furttenbach, utilizing Serlian wings of the Late Renaissance. These illustrations show the ground plan and functional design for a *telari* (periaktoi) stage. The ground plan suggests the dimensions for the construction of the *telari* stage to be used for a comedy. The location of streets and *telari* buildings is shown, together with the pin settings on which the *telari* turn and the grooves in which the back shutters are to be moved on and off stage. The graph drawing is a frontal view of the raised stage and raised shutter grooves in the back with *telari* in a new position following a scene change. The functional sketch demonstrates the clockwise and counterclockwise rotation of the *telari* on opposite sides of the stage, while the rear scene is changed by the movement of shutters placed in grooves and rolled on wheels. From the duke's seat it is all a very fascinating *changement à vue*. L. Simonson, *op. cit.*

Figure 17.   Parigi, Setting for *Il Solimano.* 1620 (Metropolitan Museum of Art), indicating flat wings in painted three-dimensional perspective and painted back shutter with vanishing point in the distance. The design is also reminiscent of Parigi's work with Aleotti at the Farnese. L. Simonson, *op. cit.*

a single understage machine which could move all the wings simultaneously at the flick of a lever (cf. 68-69 for use by G. Burnacini). A later version of the Torelli device is shown in the illustration of a seventeenth century stage (Figure 18). Succeeding illustrations (Figures 19-20) indicate the manner in which wing settings and scene changing had developed since the Serlian wings of the Late Renaissance (p. 27) and Manneristic periods. Stages would now not only be longer, but they would be more mechanized and be accompanied by increasingly deeper understage areas for housing the scenery and machines. Such changes in aesthetic concepts, construction, and engineering were outstanding marks of baroque theatre culture.

Characteristics of High Baroque Theatre

But what in particular may be said of baroque theatre art in the second half of the seventeenth century? Constructing any complete picture, even in outline, of theatre culture during this period is no small task. In addition to innumerable individual studies, complains Kindermann, research fol-

Figure 18.   Designs and model of a 17th century stage, owned by the library of the Paris Opera. cf. also Figure 15 from the *Traité de Scènographie* (1776) for the manner in which Torelli unified the scene changing by the use of a single machine, located under the stage and operated manually. Illustration by Sonrel. Paris: *Bibliothèque de l'Opera.* Exact origin of the model unknown. L. Simonson, *op. cit.*

Figure. 19.

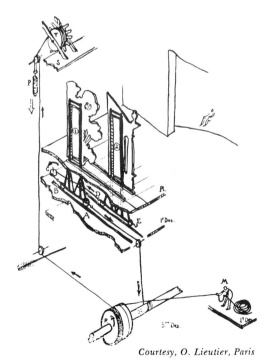

lowing the discovery of the baroque phenomenon has by no means kept pace in the various countries concerned and affected by baroque influences. The range of literature in English concerning baroque theatre has remained significantly limited.[8] Nevertheless, some features seem to distinguish German Baroque theatre quite consistently from renaissance theatre, just as this latter is inconceivable in the form of Medieaval Gothic. A technical feature, which the preserved illustrations show to a high degree, is the influence stemming from the researches of Francis Bacon, Johannes Kepler, René Descartes, and Sir Isaac Newton into the science of optics.[9] For heightened optical effect, continental baroque performances sought to contrast a darkened auditorium with a well lighted stage. At least such seems to have been the case in the German states, where baroque artists were greatly concerned to present the audience with a forceful impression, immediate, and overpowering.[10] The problem of arranging this contrast in auditorium and stage lighting, which by modern standards was still in a relatively primitive state of technological development, seems to have been resolved by starting the performances in daylight, perhaps in the afternoon, and continuing them into the night. Outdoor performances would be concluded near midnight with a huge display of fireworks in order to achieve a most impressive, contrasting, baroque close to the show.[11] Although Meyer is chiefly concerned with performances in garden and grotto theatres, illustrations of performances in theatre buildings would seem to indicate that a general custom prevailed in the timing of the performance; and this custom could be of use in creating the desired lighting contrasts, helped by the striking interplay of concave and convex surfaces.

Other phenomena which appear to describe baroque theatre best are that:

1. Life is theatre in a manner which correlates well with the pansophist goals of the leading educators in the period, as well as with the revival of gothic interests.
2. The world must be conceived as a stage, and the stage as including all the details of the world.
3. The prime mover and director of this world theatre is a personal God.[12]

As in baroque culture generally, so also in the theatre, the appeal of the performance was to sense-realism. What was the joy of reason and nature emphasized in the renaissance became more the excitement of reality and sense impression in the baroque. Where renaissance theatre had satisfied itself with relatively economical design of significance—except, perhaps, for the Italian world of intermediaries—and everything added was suited to the dialogue, with the symbolic gesture suited to the costuming and only the optical effect was required; baroque theatre strove for new effects by thousands of different sense appeals. Baroque Realism tended to disregard limits.[13] The conflagration and hell scenes depicting the sufferings of the damned, which Burnacini produced for Vienna, Santurini for Munich, and J. O. Harms erected in Dresden, were among the favorites of the day.

In contrast to renaissance drama, the baroque also showed far less deference to the dialogue in the performance. In the literature on baroque culture, there is not a single exception to the judgment that the texts and music for the operatic performances were external to the aesthetic forms displayed on the stage. Such shows today could be classified as *revues,* but with a decided difference, inasmuch as the contemporary revue tends to be closely related to the anticipated language habits of the audience. The baroque opera was not concerned with linguistic communication to any appreciable extent. To

[8] cf. Introduction.
[9] Heinz Kindermann, *op. cit.,* 9.
[10] Rudolf Meyer, *op. cit.,* 8, 110.
[11] *Ibid.,* 110.
[12] Heinz Kindermann, *op. cit.,* 13.
[13] *Ibid.,* 17.

hear was more important than to understand. What is more, the people *saw;* and the seeing could greatly assist the comprehension. Music and dance would complete whatever was lacking in design, costume, gesture, mask, and mime.[14]

The transition from the High and Late Renaissance to the Early Baroque came, as has been noted, by means of a transition in line emphasis.[15] Horizontal dimensions gave place to an increasing emphasis on vertical ones. The influences of Michelangelo, Raffael, the Venetian schools of the 1580's, El Greco and Bernini had played a large role in establishing the new direction. Moreover a dynamic inventiveness in stage designing, initiated by Aleotti and Parigi, had effected the invention and triumph of the wing and shutter system with two-dimensional surfaces. In Venice, Giacomo Torelli and Giovanni Burnacini had unified the system under the control of a single, manually operated machine, permitting immediate *changement à vue* with staging of greater depths. Henceforth, audiences could enjoy the sight of collapsing palaces, demons from the depths, angels racing onto the stage from the heavens, geniis, and deities. The means by which scene changing was effected on the new perspective stage was described earlier.[16] In High Baroque art, culturally as well as optically, vertical lines predominated, lending emphasis to the interaction and communion between here and the beyond; a matter which seemed quite stirring to baroque audiences in baroque theatres. By means of the new theatrical productions, the interplay and divergences of a three-level cosmos could be visibly demonstrated. What had been started in the Gothic designs of the late Medieval Period by means of above and below stage activity was quite modest in comparison with the power-play which could now be accomplished with the three levels. The older devices of flying a deity on an eagle, a peacock, a dragon, or on a thunder cloud were already routine technical equipment of the theater technicians and designers. With Galileo's modern science, Longhena's architectural concepts, and Torelli's machines, the entire Olympus could be glided down onto the stage. Apparatuses such as those used in *Germanico sul Reno*[17] could easily accommodate a heavenly host of fifty persons. In the religious plays of this period, the deities were not the only ones who ascended and descended. Dreams and allegories could also be demonstrated; especially in the climactic apotheosis the whole above stage suspension machines were included (Figures 20 A and B).

New solutions to problems of aesthetic space unified the whole three level action depicted by the cosmology of the baroque theature. The tension and distance needed to characterize the relationship between here and the beyond, a concept which had been developed with architectual brilliance by Baldassare Longhena in the famous *S. Maria della Salute Cathedral* between 1630 - 1651, might at last be achieved on the stage; but the accomplishment had to await the work of Ludovico O. Burnacini. In spite of brilliant machinery, Torelli seemed confined to strict, rectangular picture sections which did not especially deepen the stage. Whether he used an inner stage is not at all certain from the existing evidence. But at the *Theater auf der Cortina,* states Hans Tintelnot, the fore- and practicable middle-stages were combined within the total axial space. This new synthesis of space through motion which could unify inner- with the down-stage action, as well as that resulting from the flexible use of the three levels, complemented by a style of subordinating the choral direction to the advantage of the total architectual effect, had not previously existed and certainly had not existed in the earlier designs of L. O. Burnacini.[18]

---

[14] *Ibid.,* 18.

[15] cf. 11 - 17.

[16] cf. 23 - 25 with accompanying illustrations.

[17] Simon T. Worsthorne, *op. cit.,* illus. of undecorated machinery. Also, OSUTC film no. 1703, 3 - 4.

[18] Hans Tintelnot, *Barocktheater und Barocke Kunst* (Berlin: Verlag Gebr. Mann, 1939); OSUTC film no. 122, 56 - 57.

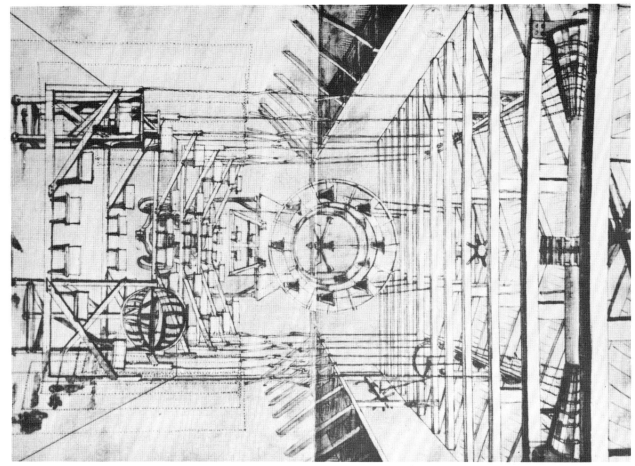

Figure 20A. *Germanico sul Reno*. Undecorated Machinery.

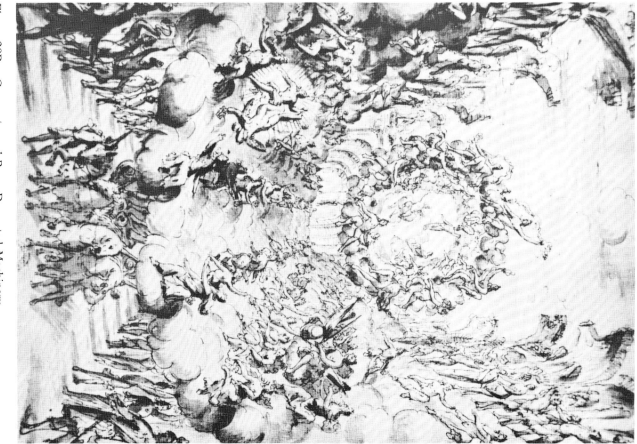

Figure 20B. *Germanico sul Reno*. Decorated Machinery.

The object which becomes valid for this dramatic battlefield with its struggle of the higher and lower powers is the individual baroque hero of courage and magnanimity.[19] The concepts valid to the designed action, therefore, become totally distinct from previous dramatic forms, diverging considerably from the ancient as well as the renaissance rules of drama and tragedy. On the same principle of unique structure, the main consequence of the baroque theatrical performance is not "Victory," but "Redemption." The individual hero does not conquer Reality; rather is the Truth of his exaltation discovered, or revealed. For the same reason, the resolution of the baroque drama is never the outcome of a subjective, free-will decision; the goal of the action has been predestined and foreordained from all eternity, to use the theological terms favored by that age.[20] Baroque theatre, consequently, is a unified art form, the purpose of which is reverence and obedience to the Absolute as the source of all power and grace. But the Absolute so worshipped is not believed to be irrational; he is the personification of the Supreme Reason that governs all reality and existence. Philosophically, Reason, as typically set forth in the continental Rationalism of Descartes and Leibniz, becomes more important than the deity using it. Thus baroque art tends to undermine its religious assumptions and create its own downfall.

In summary, we have delineated the features in the development of the German baroque theatre by noting:

1. The changes in fine art, music, and theatre which helped to create the cultural atmosphere of the baroque age.
2. The conditions, features, and ideals which seemed crucial to the development of German baroque culture.
3. The characteristics which appear to distinguish baroque theatre productions from earlier forms in the history of theatre.

Similarly, the next chapter will deal mainly with the history of theatre at the Viennese Imperial Court.

---

[19] cf. 5 - 10.

[20] R. Alewyn, "Vom Geist des Barocktheaters," *Weltliteratur Festgabe für Fritz Strich* (Bern, Switzerland, 1952), 24.

3

The Growth of Baroque
Theatre at Vienna

Cultural Prelude under Ferdinand II

The ascendancy of baroque opera at the Imperial Court received its first strong impulse under the rulership of Ferdinand III (1637 - 1657). Emperor Maximilian and his successors had always been great lovers of music. Ferdinand II (1619 - 1637) had accounted music as a prime factor in the education of the prince.

Notwithstanding the financial difficulties and material destruction of The Thirty Years' War, elaborate festivities were ordered for the marriage of Ferdinand III to the Spanish Infantin Maria. The performance of a comedy by Pedro Calderón de la Barca was included. Also, for the first time at Vienna, ballets came to be mentioned. To celebrate the wedding, a festival train went through the streets, bearing nymphs on six wagons pulled by white horses, "deer," and "unicorns."[1] Following the nymph bearing wagons were Neptune with twenty whales from which numerous reed flutes could be heard, a garden of Venus with flowers and a fountain with running water, and a final wagon with a mountain on which a comedy was enacted. A horse ballet was also introduced, during which the riders moved their horses into a formation spelling out the names Ferdinand and Maria. The wedding festivities concluded with a court masque and ballet in which the members of the royal family assumed the character roles of mythological heroes and gods.[2]

These events, however, were but a small prelude suggesting the greater things to come. With Ferdinand III, the movement of Baroque opera was first introduced to Vienna. Concerning the versatile

---

[1] Andreas Liess, *Wiener Barockmusik* (Wien: Verlag L. Doblinger (B. Herzmansky, 1946), 63.   [2] *Ibid.,* 63.

emperor, his brother Archduke Wilhelm wrote that he supported his sceptre with a lyre and a sword.[3] He also begins the series of the four composing emperors, to which Leopold I, Josef I, and Karl VI belong.

After 1640, numerous Italian operas began to find their way to the Imperial Court at Vienna. Favorite performance places were the Hofburg ballroom and the Tummelplatz, now called the Joseph-platz. Outstanding and well-known composers placed their works at the disposal of the Viennese Court. The best Italian architects of the time were also sought and well paid for their then little known designs of swirling fantasy and lavish embellishment. The opera librettos, of course, would always be in the Italian language. Claudio Monteverdi became a musical adviser to the Court, where his *Arianna* was performed. Ferdinand III earnestly sought to have Monteverdi take up permanent residence in Vienna, but to no avail. In return for this generosity, Monteverdi showed his own magnanimity by presenting the emperor the special gift of his opera, *Odysseus Returns Home.* A disciple of Monteverdi, Franz Cavelli, also sent his dramatic creations to the new leading town of the Holy Roman Empire. Emperor Ferdinand III, himself, composed an allegorical drama on love, earthly and heavenly. The leading musical director of the Viennese baroque upsurge, however, was the Court choir director, Anton Bertoli.[4]

Scarcely three months after the 1651 wedding of Ferdinand III and Eleanore Gonzaga, the empress requested a comedy by the court musicians in honor of the emperor's birthday. The dialogue was to be spoken in the Italian language. Shortly thereafter, the emperor succeeded in persuading the leading architect of Mantua, Giovanni Burnacini (1610-1655), to move to Vienna as chief architect for the Imperial Court. On a previous meeting in Italy, Giovanni Burnacini had accepted an offer from Ferdinand III to build the first opera house in Vienna. The offer seems to have been sufficiently encouraging for Giovanni to bring with him his mother, brother, and soon to be famous son, Ludovico Burnacini (1636-1707). Quite possibly Ferdinand III had become acquainted with Giovanni Burnacini and his talented work during a trip to Mantua in 1649.[5] Now in Vienna, Giovanni Burnacini had the task of constructing an attractive, elegant theatre at the *Corte Cesarea.* It was to be ready for the performance of *La Gara* (The Contest), with text by Vimina and music by Bertoli, in January, 1652. The occasion was the birth of the Spanish Infantin Margarita. The opera, to be discussed in detail later, was performed in the newly constructed theatre and seems to have met with very good response. In 1651, Ferdinand III had planned to have an elaborate stage erected at his country estate; but the plans were postponed because of a death.

His architecture and scenery for *La Gara* having attained notable fame, Giovanni Burnacini was commissioned to create designs and functional set pieces for *Daphne,* performed the following month during the Fasching celebrations. The performance rivalled that of *La Gara* for good repute. Success brought more assignments for Giovanni, and he was commissioned to display his theatrical power along with the other games and science-magic which thrilled the gathering of German princes and nobles called together by Ferdinand III for a year of political consultation at Regensburg in 1653.[6] To show the conference the significance of the theatre for welding political and cultural unity, Ferdinand III had Giovanni Burnacini construct a theatre at Regensburg for the performance of *L'inganno*

[3] *Ibid.,* 63. "Er stützte sein Szepter auf Leier und Schwert."

[4] *Ibid.,* 64; Kindermann, *op. cit.,* 490-491.

[5] Flora Biach-Schiffmann, *Giovanni und Ludovico Burnacini, Theater und Feste am Wiener Hofe* (Wien and Berlin: Krystall Verlag, 1931); OSUTC film no. 123, 1-15.

[6] Abraham Wolf, *A History of Science, Technology, and Philosophy* (New York: MacMillan, 1935); Martha Ornstein, *The Role of Scientific Societies in the Seventeenth Century* (Chicago, Illinois: The University of Chicago Press, 1938), 170-175.

d'amore. Records of this theatre show that it was a two gallery auditorium of wood construction, having 60 boxes and costing 13,218 fl., said to be quite a sizeable sum for any theatre of that time. The figures and description are more than of passing interest, however, for they help to pinpoint the origin of the Tummelplatz Theatre erected by Ludovico O. Burnacini at Vienna in 1660. Persuasive evidence shows that the Regensburg Theatre had been dismantled, shipped 150 miles down the Danube to Vienna, where it was stored in autumn, 1653, and later reconstructed at the Tummelplatz.[7]

Although the *Pietas victrix* opera by Avancini, performed at the Jesuit controlled University of Vienna, bears all the marks of the Giovanni Burnacini designing style, it is not certain that this show was his last masterpiece. Following his death in 1655, Giovanni Burnacini was succeeded in his position as first court architect by his son, Ludovico. Ludovico's first term was short lived, however; for Ferdinand III died in 1657 and was succeeded by Leopold I, who brought with him a whole new set of court personnel, including a new court architect, Giovanni B. Angelini. Angelini served in the capacity of court architect for less than two years, being dismissed at the end of December, 1658. After January 1, 1659, Ludovico O. Burnacini was returned to the position of first court architect to Leopold I. The era of Ferdinand III, which had extended almost a decade beyond the Peace of Westphalia, was officially closed. The political center of the Holy Roman Empire now prepared to consolidate its positions by the elaborate exploitation of the popular High Baroque culture.

Culture and Opera Under Leopold I

The preeminence of festive opera in the cultural world of Vienna was firmly established through Leopold I, the theater-emperor. At the youthful age of seventeen, he had succeeded his father on the throne. In the midst of momentous political challenges, virtually incessant wars, competition with Louis XIV for the wealth of Spain and control of the Continent, and above all the battle against the invading Turks, Leopold I directed the ship of state for half a century. His own triumph on the Continent accompanied the fame he received for organizing the defeat and gradual explusion of the Turkish Ottoman Empire from Europe. For a moment, extended across three decades, a brilliant glory returned to the nations of The Holy Roman Empire. The renewed vigor and importance of The Holy Roman Empire was strengthened by the ascendancy of Vienna to commercial and political prominence on the Continent. The new vitality could be seen in the many new buildings of Fischer von Erlach which decorated the town. Institutes and societies were founded, art was encouraged, and even a scientific society was formed to offer some slight competition to those of England, France, and elsewhere in Europe. Whether due to this international competition, the insatiable curiosity of the baroque man who enjoyed sensational science shows, other causes, or simply to the influence of a religious heretic whom Leopold retained as a court physician, the emperor officially established the Academic Caesarea Leopoldina in 1687. This new academy of science had a rank equal to that of the University of Vienna.[8]

---

[7] Court Account Book, 1653, 560 v. Hrn. Johann Bornacini . . . den 2. 8ber auf abbruch und hinweckführüng besagten Theatri 100fl. und den 30. Jenner Ao 1654, 150 fl. cit.; Franz Hadamowsky, *op. cit.*, 32-33; The spelling of the name is an Austrian translation for Giovanni Burnacini.

[8] Martha Ornstein, *op. cit.*, 173-174. Austrian writers on the history of Austrian education are prone to conclude that the strong emphasis on baroque art did nothing to further the cause of science and enlightenment at the University of Vienna during the seventeenth century. If this hypothesis is meant to imply that science and enlightenment were encouraged in the universities of Protestant countries, it would seem to be inconclusive. By and large science remained outside the universities until after 1750; cf. Oswald Redlich, "Universitat Wien," *Das Akademische Deutschland,* Bd. I (Berlin: C. A. Weller Verlag, 1930), 406. Other histories are listed in the bibliography.

The deepest love of Leopold I, however, was in music and the theatre. In spite of the increasing pressure of political events, which were a constant threat to The Holy Roman Empire, the more dismal the situation became, the more Leopold sought consolation in the composing of music for choral performance. After referring to an increase in the death rate in a letter to Countess Pötting, dated March 3, 1666, Leopold expressed the spirit which dominated his whole reign, ". . . at least we had a genuine (Fasching) festival in the chamber *(camera.),* for the dead derive no benefit from one's being sad."[9]

The emperor himself was also an accomplished musician of his time. Ebner, Bertoli, Athanasius Kircher, and J. H. Schmelzer were all his advisors in the art of composition during his lifetime. In addition to 79 compositions for use in the churches, including eight oratorios, Leopold I was very active in cooperating on opera libretti with his chapel choir director. He also composed music for nine theatrical celebrations and seventeen volumes of ballets, of which 102 dances are still in existence and owned by the *Wiener National bibliothek.*[10]

Strong support for Leopold's cultural plans came from the Jewish circles in Vienna. Such support, surprisingly enough, was in full recognition of the Counter Reformation character of the cultural activity, as well as of Leopold's own Jesuitical education. At the famous wedding festivities of 1667, which witnessed *The Contest of Air and Water* with horse-ballet by Sbarra and L. O. Burnacini, the Jewish citizens demonstrated their support of Leopold I by presenting the empress an elegant plate with a fourteen-pound silver statue of an infant on it. The emperor did not forget this impression made on him by the leading Jewish businessmen in the silver trade, nor did the empress. At his wife's request, the Jews had their wealth confiscated, and they were exiled from Vienna in 1670. But, as the emperor's financial plans floundered, the Jewish silversmiths were begged to return the following year. To encourage their return, the Jesuit Emperor, Leopold I, assured them that he would have a synagogue constructed! The Jews generally did return, increased their status and power at the Imperial Court, and had one of their members elevated to the aristocracy. To date, however, no Jewish participation has been reported in direct connection with the composing, designing, and staging of the Viennese High Baroque operas.[11]

The personnel commissioned for the actual productions of the operas constituted a unity of artistic enterprise. During the Age of Leopold I, this unity was represented by a small group of court specialists. During the Later Baroque period, under Karl VI, when the Galli-Bibienas were the leading court designers on the Continent, the labor was divided and subdivided among groups of tradesmen and professionalists. According to the estimation of Hans Tintelnot, the baroque era came to express what was probably the first essential union of a desire for living with the theatre; far beyond its close relationship with creative art, the theatre embodied the aesthetic strivings of a whole age.[12]

Drama *per se* was to remain the concern of the citizenry and of the students until around 1750. The exclusive circle of the royal court demanded nothing less than a total, operatic performance expensively decorated with musical and vocal accomplishments. Such elegant spectacles were not nor-

[9]Letter to Countess Pötting, March 3, 1666: "Diese Fasching hätt ziemlich still sein sollen wegen der Klagen, doch haben wir etliche Festl in camera gehabt, denn es hilft den Toten doch nicht, wenn man traurig ist."; cit. in Andreas Liess, *op. cit.,* 65.

[10]*Ibid.,* 65-66.

[11]*Relationis historicae semestralis continuatio Jacobi Franci.* A historical description of the most memorable events registered in Europe. (Frankfurt am Main: Sigismundi Latomi, Mäurers, and Sel. Erben. Nr. 39 Autumn Fair, 1657, to the Eastern Fair,

1658 to Nr. 102 Easter to Fall Fair, 1689); cit. in E. Vehse, *Memoirs of the Court of Austria,* I (London: H. S. Nichols, 1896), 448; W. Flemming, *op. cit.,* 47.

[12]Hans Tintelnot, *op. cit.,* Introduction: "Erst im Barock und vielleicht nur im Barock gehören Lebensgefühl und Theater wesenhalf zusammen, verkörpert das Theater weit über seine enge Verbindung mit der bildenden Kunst hinaus das Kunstwollen eines ganzen Zeitalters."

mally open to the public,[13] but only to royalty, persons in some way attached to the court, and to visit-ing aristocracy. For public admiration and education, texts with engravings were published and sold for weeks and months after the premier performance. Following a single spectacle, however, the the-atre might actually remain unused for an entire year.[14] No thought of condescending to a "run" for the public, or for the court coffers, was ever seriously entertained by the aristocratic circles. A major assignment for the operas was the choreography, for an inspiring ballet was necessary to the grand climax and ending of the performance. Yet, an independent existence for ballet in Austria occurred only after opera had become something of a pallid attraction.

The history of theatre at the Viennese Court during the baroque era, then, was preeminently the development and elaboration of court opera. The lowly drama, acted among courtesans only by dil-ettantes of the nobility during the Fasching celebrations, was an Austrian adaptation of Commedia dell' arte forms, apparently with frequent references and allusions to early Viennese folklore.[15] Neith-er dance nor drama acquired separate existence at the Imperial Court during the period of the High Baroque. The only unified art was the festive opera, although the unity seems to have been more ex-ternal than inherent. Of course, under the leadership of Nicolaus von Avancini, Jesuit shows present-ed by the students for the public at the University Aula ascended to a level of display that sometimes rivalled the shows at the Imperial Court. Father Müller, a more recent Jesuit author, complains that the embellishments of Avancini really robbed the religious drama of its great soul and created a spirit antithetical to that of Jesuitism—the preeminence of the secular state.[16]

The chief personnel responsible for creating aesthetic unities at the court of Leopold I were Minato (text), Draghi (music), and L. O. Burnacini (architect and costumer). An exception to this trio could be made whenever Leopold himself was moved to compose music and libretti. The only person of the famed trio who lasted any great length of time at the Imperial Court was Ludovico Burnacini.

The personnel needed for the singing and acting were drawn largely from the court family, pro-fessional troupes, and subordinate court units. All servants, from the chamber maids to the cook, the youths, or the laundry maids could be ordered to perform by their superiors. Of course, any superi-or might escape his responsibility, if he could order a subordinate to take his place. But the only se-curity which the theatre artists had for their employment was the good will and survival potential of the patron. The death of the emperor resulted in immediate unemployment for all the members of the court, as was the case with the Burnacini family in 1657. A new ruler usually brought with him a com-pletely new organization, as Karl VI did in 1711, when he made Ferdinando Galli-Bibiena the chief architect of the Imperial Court.

Perhaps the most significant person for the development of written theatre history at this time was the Theatre Secretary, Giovanni Benaglia. As early as 1671, Benaglia, who was also the Court Inspector, was employed as the Theatre Secretary. He remained in this office forty years. Benaglia was succeeded by his son, Giovanni Antonio. These men have provided the historians with practical, unsensational bookkeeping records which have increased the accuracy of historical reports and have aided considerably in the understanding of the Austrian court perfromances.

---

[13]cf., 4-5.

[14]Franz Hadamowsky, *op. cit.*, 36-37.

[15]*Ibid.*, 7-8.

[16]Johannes Müller, S. J., *Das Jesuitendrama*, I (Augsburg: Dr. Benno Filser Verlag GMBH, 1930), 96.

4

Places of Performance

Having discussed the cultural atmosphere and personnel responsible for the rapid growth of baroque theatre at Vienna, something must now be said in respect to the places in and about Vienna where the flourish of baroque opera was especially noticeable (Figure 21). The places were many, for the occasions were also many. Weddings, birthdays, christenings, State visits, religious feasts were but some of the events which required celebration and dramatic performances. Among the favorite performing locations for these occasions were theatre buildings, drawing rooms, palace halls and salons, the Hofburg gardens, and the emperor's country estates.[1] Most of the performance places are either no longer identifiable or, because they were not recorded, are simply not known. But even the existing information indicates a lively calendar of theatrical events.

The earliest, and perhaps the oldest theatre auditorium on which information exists was the Salon "della Favorita." It was in this location that Amaltea's *Virtu Guerriera* was presented. Engravings of Favorita shows, however, are all from the years following the Turkish invasion. The oldest showplace at the Hofburg was probably the ballroom (Figure 22), which could be converted into a stage and auditorium within a few weeks, as was done for *La Galatea* in 1667. The ballroom had been decorated for a festival dance in 1631, honoring the Spanish Wedding. It was constructed as a palace extension, approximately on the location now occupied by the formal ballrooms. The original ballroom was about 51.3m long and 19m wide, quite large enough to house *Il Sidonio,* as well as many operas, comedies, and dances in the succeeding decade.

[1] Franz Hadamowsky, *op. cit.,* 22-30.

Figure 21.   View of Vienna toward the West, 1672. Open-air shows were often held near the surrounding villages.

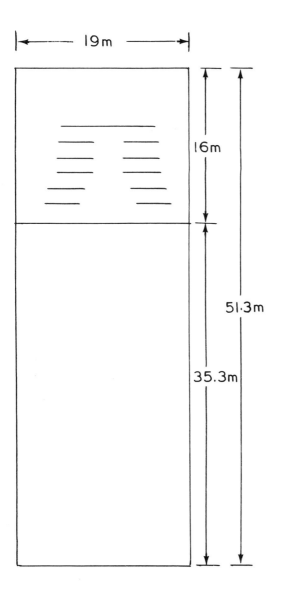

Figure 22.   Floor plan for the Hofburg Ballroom in Vienna.
Scale: 4sq. = 1m. 1m. = 39.7 in. Drawing by Robert A. Griffin,
based on data from Hadamowsky, *op. cit.*, 31.

The most significant structure of Viennese High Baroque, of course, was the *Theater auf der Cortina*. Plans for building this second court theatre were submitted in 1666, but it was not finished until the winter of 1667 - 1668. The construction delays at the Cortina were the cause of the hasty reconstruction of the ballroom for *La Galatea* in 1667.

Prior to building the Cortina, Ludovico O. Burnacini had managed to complete one other major engineering feat, the construction of a theatre at the Tummelplatz (Figure 23A). In all probability, the Tummelplatz Theatre of 1660 was a Viennese rehabilitation of Giovanni Burnacini's Regensburg Theatre of 1653. The evidence for this conclusion is as follows:

1. Both theatres had two galleries with sixty boxes.
2. Heinz Kindermann's pictorial comparison of shows at the two theatres (Figure 23A, B) offers strong circumstantial evidence that L. O. Burnacini used the same stage columns as set pieces that Giovanni Burnacini had used at Regensburg, and that the ceiling had been

Figure 23A. cf. also Figure 23B. The comparison of these two pictures strongly implies that the building in Figure A (1653) had been dismantled and shipped down the Danube River to Vienna, where it was reassembled for *La forza della fortuna e della virtu* (1661) at the Tummelplatz. The Illustrations are from Kindermann, *op. cit.* Figure A shows the decorations behind the proscenium.

only overlaid with new embellishments. Wing extensions have been added as a stage modi-
fication for the production of *La forza della fortuna e della virtu,* 1661.
3. No money was set aside for the purchase of wood in the construction, although all of the
    Viennese theatres were then of wood construction throughout.

The clear implication is that the Regensburg theatre had been dismantled and shipped down the Danube to Vienna, where it was stored in 1653, then later sent to the Tummelplatz for reconstruction.
But the building seems to have become too aged and weather-beaten for revival, for reports are that
ceiling beams of the second gallery sometimes fell on the audience, and at least one lady was seriously injured in this way.[2]
    While unfavorable weather and financial problems prevented the Cortina from being construct-
ed on schedule, the announcement came of the arrival of the Spanish Infanta, Leopold's bride-to-be.
The Cortina was earnestly desired for the wedding festivities, but the mentioned difficulties resulted in the cancellation of elaborately designed shows. The decision was made to use the inner courtyard of the Hofburg for *The Contest of Air and Water* and the ballroom for a musical pastoral, *La
Galatea.* Ludovico Burnacini was requested to design the scenery for both shows in addition to continuing his work on the Cortina. For the Cortina, he received funds in three more installments:
June, 1666; December, 1666; and September, 1667.

[2] *Ibid.,* 32. The court account books have no financial provision
for lumber supplies.

Figure 24.   "Contest between Air and Water," a festival production with horse ballet performed in the Hofburg courtyard on the occasion of Leopold's wedding, 1667.

On December 5, 1666, the Spanish Infanta Margareta Theresa, age 16, arrived in Vienna and was wedded to Leopold I. The dramatic wedding festivities (Figure 24) are recorded in the newspaper, *Frankfurter Relations.* At the Hofburg, two galleries of seats accommodated the audience. The flat area of the inner Burgplatz was used for the staging. The first day of festivities required a fireworks display, arranged by acts and scenes. The pageant procession illustrated is that which took place on the 24th and the 31st of January, 1667. For this show, a Turkish galley on a truck surrounded with water, probably artificial, was required. The weight of the ship and personnel broke the truck wheels, so that the galley was disabled for the second performance on January 31. Other wagons which were accommodated at the inner Burgplatz performance were Neptune's whale, a mountain garden to symbolize Earth, Air with rainbow, and Fire. The Earth and Air wagons had Italian singers, who for a considerable time sang praises to the empress. Also included in the performance were flying figures, dancing ensembles, and the equestrian ballet in which the emperor participated and possibly fell from his horse.[3]

To return to the Cortina, the building was completed in the winter of 1667-1668, but not before a scheduled performance of *Il pomo d'oro* arranged for February of the previous year had had to be cancelled. Finally, in July, 1668, the Cortina's long awaited opening (Figure 1) was celebrated in

[3] *Relationis historicae,* Nrs. 30-102, also called "Frankfurther Relations," cit. in E. Vehse, *op. cit.,* 444-448; *Theatrum Europaeum* X, 497, cit. by Hadamowsky, *op. cit.,* 73.

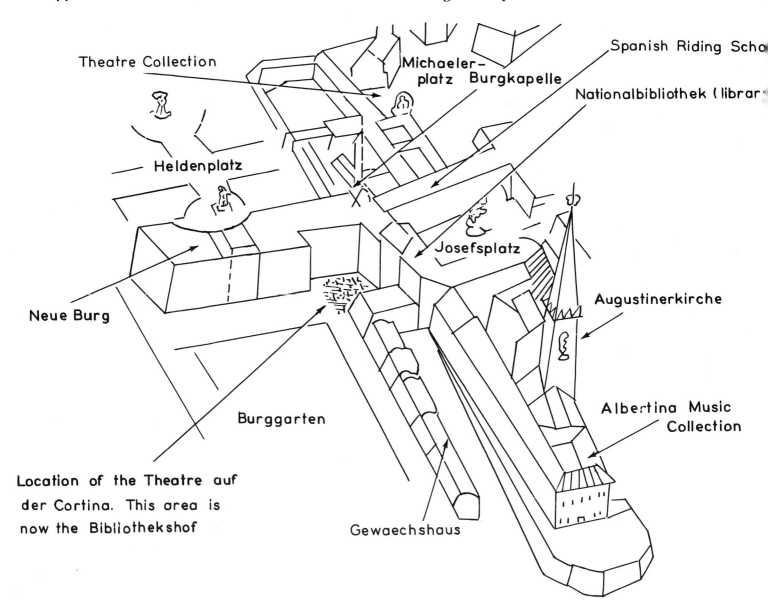

Figure 25.   The Library section of the Hofburg showing the location of the *Theater auf der Cortina.* Perspective drawing by Robert A. Griffin from an original sketch of Konrad Zobel made in Vienna, 1966.

conjunction with the birthday and festivities of Empress Margareta Theresa. The opera selected for the occasion was the previously cancelled *Il pomo d'oro.* The performance was planned for two days, July 13-14. Following the close of the show on July 14, the Spanish ambassador in attendance awarded the stars with large gifts of money.[4]

As was customary, the elaborate performance of *Il pomo d'oro* had accomplished the purpose of the construction, and the building thereafter remained empty for months at a time. Being made of wood and seldom used, the Cortina was in constant need of repair, especially from weather conditions. The *Theater auf der Cortina* was finally destroyed during the Turkish siege of Vienna on July 16, 1683. Suttinger's plan of the city, made just after the Turkish siege was broken, shows the foundation of

[4] Franz Hadamowsky, *op. cit.,* 33-37.

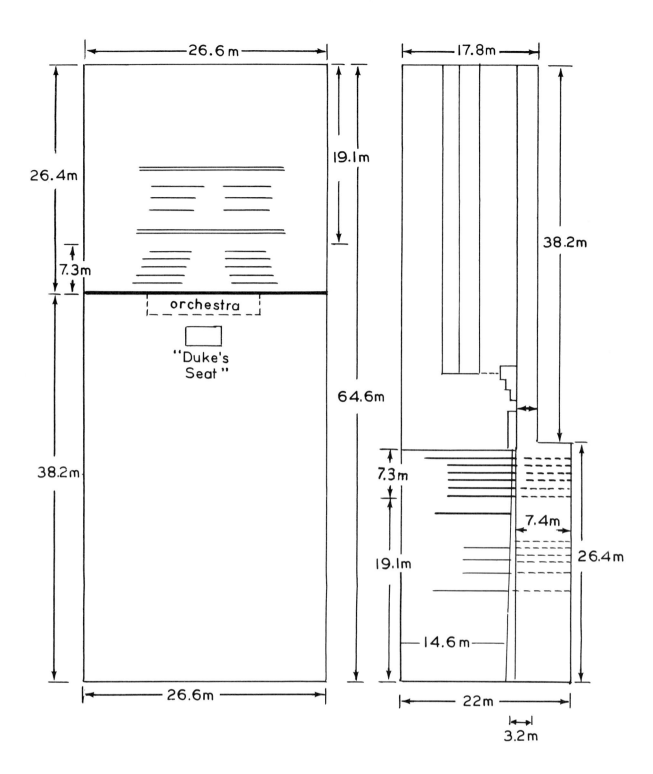

Figure 26. *Theater auf der Cortina.* Front wings c. 6.4m high. Back wings c. 3m high. Drawing by Robert A. Griffin based on data from Hadamowsky, *op. cit.,* 37.

the theatre, which was probably never rebuilt.[5] Had the Turks been more successful, the oil-soaked timbers of the Cortina would have become a rather large torch for burning the city.

By dimensions, the Cortina (Figures 25-26), was designed to be 64.6m long, 26.6m wide, and 14.6m high. The foundation for the understage area was excavated to a depth of 7.3m, but this depth

[5] Max Eisler, *Historischer Atlas* (Wien: Arbeiten des Kunsthistorisches Instituts der Universität Wien, n.d.), Bd. 16.

did not extend beyond the understage area. The excavation and construction under the auditorium was just half the depth of the understage area. In sum, adequate space was available for housing the frames, machinery, and equipment shown in the Paris Library's model of a seventeenth century theatre. A re-drawing of the Cortina, as here conjectured, admits a minimum stage raking of 20 cm.[6] The cost of the structure was 24,700 fl., or almost double the cost of the 1653 Regensburg theatre.[7]

One may reasonably hypothesize that when the Cortina was dismantled, some of the elegant operas were assigned to be performed "in the Cesarea Corte" of Giovanni Burnacini, while the less elaborate musical shows for the exclusive circles were arranged for the cruder stage of the large castle salon after 1683. Performances during the autumn, winter, and early spring were scheduled for theatres in town. During the late spring and summer, the Favorita gardens were preferred with alternate shows possible for Laxenburg, Lehndorf, Schönbrunn Castle, and grottoes at the country estates.

Information on the "King's Quarter" and on the "Queen's Quarter," as well as on other named locations for performances given between 1687 - 1694 is not now available. Information is also lacking as to whether the annual celebrations were always given in the same locations. Nevertheless, a custom adopted under Leopold I was continued under Karl VI—large theatre for the operas honoring the emperor's birthday, and small theatre for the Fasching operas.[8] Public shows were given at the University Aula.

Garden Shows at the Favorita

At the Favorita Garden a wealth of theatrical life went on. This location is now Vienna IV, the Favoritenstrasse. The Turks razed this theatre in 1683, but, following the death of his stepmother, Eleanore Gonzaga, Leopold I had the Favorita rebuilt by L. O. Burnacini during the period 1687 - 1691. The succeeding emperors, Josef I and Karl VI, were also to use the Favorita as an annual summer palace. After attending an opera at this pond-theatre as designed under the direction of Ferdinando Galli-Bibiena (Figure 27A and B), Lady Montagu wrote as follows to a close acquaintance on September 14, 1716:

> Nothing of that kind ever was more magnificent; and I can easily believe what I am told, that the decorations and habits cost the emperor thirty thousand pounds sterling. The stage was built over a wry large canal and, at the beginning of the second act, divided into two parts, discovering the water, on which there immediately came, from different parts, two fleets of little gilded vessels, that gave the representation of a naval fight . . . The story of the opera is the enchantment of Alcina, which gives opportunity for a great variety of Machines, and changes of scenes, which are performed with a surprising swiftness. The theatre is so large that it is hard to carry the eye to the end of it . . . No house could hold such large decorations.[9]

The Favorita had a comedy-salon in the north quarter, which is now the front side along the Taubstummengasse; the diagonal side being the first four windows in the Favoritenstrasse, as one approaches from the city. Additionally, the gallery, the long salon, and the second ante-chamber were used for shows.

In fact, whenever theatrical celebrations could at all be held in a palace of the emperor, the Favorita was preferred. Palace and garden were justly assigned their name, for the Favorita was the most

[6] cf. Figure 26.

[7] Franz Hadamowsky, *op. cit.,* 37.

[8] *Ibid.,* 40.

[9] Mary Wortley Montagu, *Letters and Works,* I (London: 1837), 285.

Figure 27 A and B.   Stage designs by Ferdinando and Giuseppe Galli-Bibiena for *Angelica, Vincitrice Di Alcina;* libretto by Pariati, music by Fux; performed at the Favorita, 1716 (Kinderman, *op. cit.*)

cherished estate of the emperor. Even before the siege and destruction by the Turks (1683), a wealth of drama and festivities had taken place in the pleasant little palace on the meadow. Although very many comedies, operas, serenades, and choral programs were performed in the salons of the Favorita, existing records seldom indicate a specific location for the construction of the stage or auditorium. Nor does the manner of the performance offer much evidence on the problems of auditorium and staging. A few inferences may be drawn, however, from performances which were specifically for the Favorita Garden.

On October 15, 1673, the opera *Provare per non recitare* was performed, with libretto by Minato and music by Draghi. The scenery was probably by L. O. Burnacini. The scenery for the Minato-Draghi *Il Monte Chimara* opera in 1682 is likewise not recorded. The destructions of the Turkish siege had been so extensive that in spite of Burnacini's efforts, almost a decade was needed to make the Favorita once more suitable for operatic performances. The landscaping and the replanting of the garden was assigned to a Frenchman, Jean Trehet. By 1698, elegant performances were again being held at the Favorita, and they probably surpassed the performances prior to the war by no small degree. On the occasion of the emperor's birthday in 1698, the Draghi musical work *Il delizio Ritiro di Lucullo* was given with accompanying scenery. In the Burnacini style, a palace was represented so that the Favorita Garden itself became the Garden of Lucullus in the imagination of the audience. The

Figure 28. *L'Euleo Festigiante nel Ritorno d'Alessandro Magno dall' Indie.* The music was Giovanni Bononcini, with scenery by Ludovico Burnacini.

garden was conceived as directly adjoining the entrance to the palace. A person could step through the palace entrance into the garden of Lucullus.[10]

In the following year the birthday of Prince Josef I was celebrated in a colorful manner. In the garden of the Favorita a "serenade" was played, which carried the title, *L'Euleo Festigiante nel Ritorno d' Alessandro Magno dall' Indie.* The music was by Giovanni Bononcini, with scenery by Ludovico Burnacini. The preface to the text called for a garden scene with a beautifully designed edifice, a majestic fountain, and night illumination.[11] The last scene of this performance (Figure 28), has been preserved in one of Burnacini's own engravings.[12] Between the audience, seated semi-circularly at the front of the theatre, and the brightly lighted palace scene was an excavated pond. In Burnacini's engraving, the background enclosure of columns seems to open to an infinite depth, surrounded by arcades and arches with a cloud-covered path in the distance, composing the setting for the ballet to be performed.[13]

In the year 1700 the birthday of Leopold I was celebrated with similar festivities. The opera *La Costanza d'Ulisse* was performed (Figure 29). Again the scenery was from L. O. Burnacini. The text

[10] Musiksammlung der Albertina, Partitur 16011, and for the following discussion nos. 407, 371; 406, 744; 406, 762; 164, 874. Also Rudolf Meyer, *op. cit.*, 101-103.

[11] "Apparato: nella Peschiera del Cesarea Giardino della Favorita si vede un vago e sotuoso edificio di bellissima architettura, e di maestuoso lavoro, con gran magnificenza illuminato di notte,

il quale si figura un delizio Palagio sopra un isolette de fiume Euleo."

[12] Flora Biach-Schiffman, *op. cit.*, 121.

[13] *Ibid.*, 121. The clouds were probably intended to be natural. No evidence exists for the use of flying machines in Viennese open-air shows.

Figure 29. *La Costanza d'Ulisse.* at the Favorita Gardens of Vienna, 1770. The main stage is the garden of Circe; the inner stage is a floating island, symbolizing the transformed ship of Ulysses. Shadows are shown in connection with the dancers, but no cause is assigned for the phenomenon.

description calls for an elegant garden setting by a lake where Ulysses wages a naval campaign.[14] The text contains two engravings from Burnacini which suggest the setting for the action. In the first, the desolate cliffs of a mountain island are shown, on which the Greeks battle against animal monstrosities.[15] The second, Figure 29, indicates tall, painted wings on both sides of a narrow elevation to the rear of a pond. The construction of the frame-wings extends right and left to wall wings at the sides of the middle stage, which in turn progress by wall frames downstage, to where they are fastened to high footwalls on the forestage. From the upstage center position of the pond, an island seems to be floating, on which rows of cypress run on to a vanishing point. It is intended to be the Greek ship which has been transformed into a garden island. Special lighting, however, is not called for in the script. Yet the shadows are so arranged that only the stage seems to be lighted. No final solution now exists for this paradox. A legitimate hypothesis might be that the show was to take place in the late afternoon, toward sunset, unless Burnacini just liked to decorate his engravings with light and shadow.

In the following year, another evening performance with special lighting did occur and was so recorded. The opera *Gli Ossequi della Notte* with music by Ziani and scenery by Burnacini specifically designates the use of nighttime illumination. This is described in the preface to the text.[16] The same performance was repeated on July 15, 1709, in honor of the christening of Princess Amalie Wilhelmina. According to a further note of 1706, a serenade of P. A. Bernadoni at the Favorita grotto was given under lighting provided by many pipe-lights. The show was *Armino*, with music by Antonio Bononcini.[17]

Outside of Vienna numerous open-air shows were held in gardens other than the Favorita. At the Imperial Gardens of Graz, in 1673, the Minato and Draghi opera *G'Incantesimi discolti, introduzione d'un Balletto* was performed. The scenery likewise was from L. O. Burnacini.[18] Also to be mentioned is a performance said to have taken place at the castle garden of Frostorff in 1681. The work was *Rivalita nell Ossequio* by an anonymous author.

Considered on the whole, and according to principles of theatrical staging, the outdoor performances fall into three groups:

1. The huge plastic constructions of unified scenery, having little scene change, and being in little relationship to the environs of the theatre;
2. The varied and rich scene transformations of well equipped pond theatres, which also bore little relationship to the whole garden;
3. Designs which required the participation of the garden elements either to modify the scene or to be set in some significant relation to the scene. Designs which made the gardens all or even the main elements in the setting probably did not occur in the seventeenth century. No one ever seems to have attempted such a creation as placing a stage in the cen-

---

[14] "Nella Peschiera del Cesareo Giardino della Favorita, che si figurerà un picciol braccio del Mar Tireno apparierà un asprissimo scoglio, sparso di precipizie, e pieno di vari mostri. Poi si cangerà in un delicioso Giardino, nel quale i sudetti mostri si muteranno in Amori. Di lontano si vedrà la nave de'campagni d'Ulisse con Telemaco già cangiata da Circa in una medisima Scena."; cit. in Biach-Schiffmann, 39.

[15] *Ibid.*, illus. 39.

[16] *Ibid.*, "Sopra la Peschiera del Cesareo Giardino della Favorita si vede un' Anfiteatro d'ingegnosa architettura, adorno di vague Piramidi, e pomposamente illuminato."

[17] Johannes Schwarz, *Die kaiserliche Sommerresidenz Favorita auf der Wieden in Wien* (Wien und Prag, 1899), 36: "unter Beleuchtung vieler Windlichter." Primary evidence for this conclusion is uncertain.

[18] Rudolf Meyer, *op. cit.*, 106, and ftnt. 100: "Die Liste der Texte, zu denen Burnacini nachweislich die Dekorationen geschaffen hat, welche Biach-Schiffmann . . . zusammenstellt, ist unvollständig. Ausser den *Incantesimi* fehlen auch noch andere Werke."

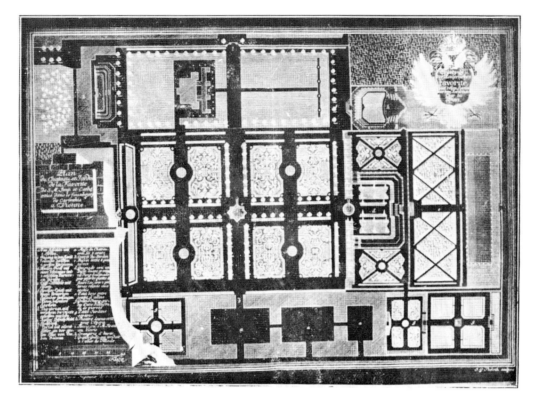

Figure 30.   Plan for the layout of the Favorita Garden, c 1730 (engraving by Solomon Kleiner).

ter of a garden where the walks and hedges came together in the form of a star, as was the case later at Schönbrunn Castle, so that the stage served as an axial perspective into the garden walks.

To return briefly to the question of the Favorita garden theatre, a plan exists which shows both the arrangement of the garden and the form of the theatre (Figure 30). Unfortunately, the plan seems to be after 1730, and the theatre design seems to have been attached to the document as an afterthought.[19] No evidence exists, either, that such a theatre as the one suggested on the garden plan was constructed and used after 1730. As a hypothetical floor plan to the designs of Burnacini, the unique little sketch is of some interest.

In this chapter, consideration has been given to the preparations, personnel, and places which account for the flourishing of High Baroque theatre at the Imperial Court during the last half of the seventeenth century.

The events may be summarized as follows:

1. Under the rule of Ferdinand III, the operas of Claudio Monteverdi and Franz Cavelli were performed with lavish display at the Imperial Court. The leading court architect in this period was Giovanni Burnacini.
2. High Baroque opera received its strongest encouragement from Leopold I. The Emperor, in turn, received considerable support for his cultural projects from the Jewish community.

[19] *Ibid.,* 113 - 114.

3. The theatrical productions were a unity of enterprise.
4. The personnel for the performances were drawn from the Court.
5. Favorite places of performance were the Hofburg, the *Theater auf der Cortina,* the *Tummelplatz,* and the *Favorita.*

Attention will now be given to the leading designers of the period. Subsequently, a detailed analysis will be given of a few of the works which owe their significance to wide acclaim.

Part II:
Architects of Viennese
High Baroque Culture

5

P. Nicolaus Avancini

Theatre history during the High Baroque period in Vienna is dominated by three names: P. Nicolaus Avancini, a Jesuit professor at the university, Giovanni Burnacini, and Ludovico O. Burnacini. The last mentioned name is perhaps the most widely known, but his fame is not to be dissociated from the foundations laid by his two predecessors. In order to build a more comprehensive picture of the High Baroque culture reflected in the outstanding opera of the period, *Il pomo d'oro,* it is worthwhile to consider the work of these three cultural giants in the order mentioned.

Since 1620 the Jesuit order had possessed a stage in one of the university buildings bordering the courtyard of the school. In 1650, additions of a large stage and a small stage were provided in the new rooms of the college at the University Place. Again, a sum of money reaching to three columns of figures was given by Leopold I for the renovation of the university courtyard stage in 1674. Altogether, Leopold I, himself educated by the Jesuits, encouraged a close relationship between the elegant court operas and the scenic forms developed in the university performances. In this effort, Leopold received much cooperation from the nobility and members of the court, who attended and lavished gifts upon the work being conducted by Nicolaus Avancini. In point of fact, this mood of support was already well under way with the end of the Thirty Years' War, or some two years before Giovanni Burnacini was commissioned to build the Cesarea Corte Theatre.[1]

---

[1] Kindermann, *op. cit.,* 452. A cover page to the Vienna University matriculation bulletin of 1648 bears a marked resemblance to the scenic potential of N. Avancini. The setting for the design is an adaptation of a Jesuit proscenium staging. *600 Jahre Universität Wien* (Wien: Osterreichischer Bundes-Verlag für Unterricht, Wissenschaft und Kunst, 1965), opp. 18.

Nicolaus Avancini (1611 - 1686) was officially the university professor for philosophy and rhetoric. But his poetry was so greatly appreciated by Ferdinand III and Leopold I that Avancini was raised to the position of a veritable court poet to be accompanied by Sbarra in 1665. Born in the Italian seaport of Trieste, Avancini had received his education in Graz, Austria. Following the completion of his studies in Graz, Avancini had already distinguished himself as a teacher, poet, playwright, and theatre director, before being called to the University of Vienna. In Vienna, he continued to publish a series of religious and patriotic odes, as well as panegyric songs in honor of the emperor whom he served. As a special tribute to Leopold I, Avancini composed a book of moral philosophy, stated in fifty odes, and presented it to the emperor on behalf of the Vienna University.[2]

The theatre work of Avancini at the University Aula presented a series of unique problems. To carry through the aims and encouragement of the Imperial Court for the university he would have to meet the following requirements:

1. Offer an artistic and dramatic media for making Jesuit character and social values important to the public in the new operatic form.
2. Retain the use of Latin in the dialogue while rendering its meaning clear by scenery and action.
3. Develop a comprehensible performance from actors who may have had no previous knowledge of Latin.
4. Implement the performance as an artistic unity.

Beginning with his festival play, *Zelus sive Franciscus Xaverus* (1640), Avancini soon advanced to more decorative plays. His theatrical achievements were to be known as the *Ludi Caesarei. Clodoaldus* (1647) and the peace play, *Joseph* (1650), had already approximated the *Ludi Caesarea* type quite closely. The type reached its most mature expression with *Pietas victrix* (1659). It was this play more than any other Jesuit performance that represented the intoxicating elegance of the new self-importance in baroque catholicism, which has been described earlier.[3] Dance and song, highly embellished rhetoric and elaborately decorated scenery, banquets, duels, and ship scenes were all woven into a unified operatic performance, a panegyric art work which culminated in a song of praise by the Holy Helen in honor of all the Habsburg rulers from Rudolf I to Leopold I, who were recognized by the Roman Catholics as the successors of the Roman emperor, Constantine. Again, in keeping with the spirit of baroque culture, the dramatic effect was not developed from an element of conflict in the dialogue or action, but was to be experienced in the glory of God being revealed through the opening clouds, which descended from above stage.

Leopold I had real use for the cultural values expressed on the Jesuit stage in the elegant baroque manner he encouraged so much. In fact, the religious and missionary goal was subordinated to the political consolidation efforts of the absolute ruler. The *Ludi Caesarei* of the Avancini era, as well as the expensively designed plays of the following decades, climaxed their religious plots in a glorious revelation of Habsburg dynasty. For assistance in this enterprise, Leopold and his successors placed the most famous painters and composers of the age at the disposal of the Jesuit theatre managers. When the Swedes invaded the Holy Roman Empire of the Habsburgs in 1642, Avancini composed his *Fiducia in Deum sive Bethulia liberata* to strengthen the religious faith and political loyalty of the populace. In an allegorical play concerning the liberation of Bethulia by Judith, the oppressive antagonist, Holo-

[2] *Ibid.*, 452.   [3] cf. 5-7.

fernes, became a deliberate personification of the plundering Swedish officers. The attacks of this kind of oppressor, alleged Avancini, were not sufficient cause for one to become discouraged. In a later play, intended to celebrate The Peace of Westphalia in 1648, Avancini chose as his allegorical title, *Pax imperii anni Domini 1650 sive Joseph a fratribus recognitus.* The reconciliation of Joseph and his brothers in Egypt depicts the redemption of the nations through their rulers at the close of the Thirty Years' War, which had brought an entire continent to the verge of destruction.[4]

In the forty years of his professorial duties, which ultimately took him to Rome as an educational leader, Avancini composed thirty-three dramatic pieces, designing virtually all of them himself. In the case of *Pietas victrix,* however, *a possibility exists that at least some of the decorations were by Giovanni Burnacini.* This question will be taken up again later. Twenty-seven of the dramatic pieces are contained in his five volumes of *Poesis dramatica.* Through Avancini, the University Aula Theatre was transformed into a modern, baroque wing and shutter stage. Whatever was to be depicted— biblical plots, allegories, martyr shows, legends, or historical dramas—seems never to have proceeded from a central heroic figure or from an element of conflict inherent to the action. Avancini's measure of theatrical effect seems always to have been dependent on the dramaturgical structure. The characterization and scenic formation were arranged in climactic order for a maximum of optical and acoustical effect. The suspense could be heightened by having some of the scenes move more slowly, or by retarding the sequence at chosen intervals by stage business. The most desirable climax would occur at the psychological moment when all the technical and mechanical wizardry, combined with scenic adornment, was directed from many sides at the audience. The Burnacini creations, which were being developed for the Viennese baroque opera, were readily assimilated by N. Avancini; only Avancini and the theatre of the University Aula differed from the court operas through an extensive use of inflated and embellished language. Otherwise, music and dance in the operatic style, which was so popular in the private court shows, became requisite parts of Avancini's artistic synthesis. The Jesuit educator Johnnes Müller had definite reasons to complain more recently that the dramaturgical designs of Avancini provided an artificial, secular substitute for the religious probings of the soul which had characterized the Jesuit shows up to his time.[5]

The theme of *Pietas victrix, sive Flavius Constantinus Magnus de Maxentio Tyranno Victor* is the conquest of Constantine over the material and spiritual forces of tyranny. The forces of tyranny are represented by Maxentius and his warriors. The basis of Constantine's victory is his faith and piety toward the promise of conquest given him by the apostolic guardians of Rome, Peter and Paul. The end of the struggle, which spells defeat for Maxentius and the powers of hell, is climaxed in the establishment of the Holy Roman Empire by Constantine and his son, who naturally becomes the heir to the throne. But the glory scene at the close is topped by the double-eagle, symbol of the Habsburg House. The dramatic metaphor would seem to instruct the audience that the victory of Constantine and his piety constitute the principles for the Christian basis of the Habsurg Empire.

The analysis of this dramatic piece brings some interesting production problems to light. Factors which might well be expected to be of importance to this show were the tendency toward deeper staging, wing and shutter scenery, machinery, music and ballet, and the use of stock characters in the performance.

Considering first *the stage,* one might note that the Aula stage for *Pietas victrix* differed greatly from the stage available for the premier performance of *Cenodoxus* at Augsburg in 1602. Espe-

---

[4] Kindermann, *op. cit.,* 454.   [5] Johannes Müller, *op. cit.,* 96.

cially with the *Ludi Caesarei* of the Avancini era, the full, deep dimension of the stage space was required. In place of a shallow multiple set, so popular in the fifteenth century, a stage had been developed with five rows of wings and a shutter area, which could be quickly changed in full view of the audience, and the wing stage could have differing degrees of depth for varying the scene changes. An ornately decorated proscenium opening was architecturally unified with an auditorium which could accommodate about two thousand persons. The University Aula stage viewed by these spectators was approximately on a level with the second gallery. To the right and left of the proscenium opening were two imposing statues of soldiers on horseback. Above the proscenium arch were two double-eagles, holding the sceptre, sword, and empire-apple, along with the portraits of Leopold I and two other members of the royal family.[6]

The stage decorations were defined by the limits of the wing and shutter system. If only the fore-stage was used, then the farthest extent of stage was closed off by painted shutters moved together onto the center of the stage, as one moves sliding doors. Furttenbach had already described these panels quite precisely. They were being widely used in Europe and England to create an uninterrupted flow of scene changing through an alternate use of fore- and inner-stage which did not necessitate the drawing of the curtain on the forestage. In this way, several scene changes became possible within any one Act. But even more importantly, an especially well painted piece of scenery might in this manner be allowed to appear in the middle of an Act, and then be made to disappear again. As the performance continued on the forestage, with a shutter closing off the deeper areas, the painted perspective and set pieces were changed on the inner stage. For example, the dream of Constantine in *Pietas victrix* requires the inner-stage for its full setting, but, when awake in the following scene, Constantine speaks his monologue on the forestage. Likewise, at the start of the Third Act the design for the full hell scene does not appear; when an announcement is made by two fleeing demons—"panditur Infernus . . ."—hell suddenly opens. Many of these Viennese Jesuit scenes of the High and Late Baroque periods extend to as many as 12 to 15 alternating changes in a single show. Almost always, these stage decorations require a throne room, several chamber scenes with each one more ornate than the preceding one, a courtyard, a temple, a forest, a courtly estate, a street in a marketplace, a desert, hell, and definitely a coastal scene with high, rugged cliffs rising above movable water. Through the waves one can also move ships, tritons, and mermaids. Since these moving optical elements and their relationships to musical compositions were inadequate to satisfy the sense-realism of the baroque era, acoustical pictures were also suggested: most prominent among these were bird songs, owl screeching, bellowing hounds, thunderstorms, and blaring trumpets. Such were the available means for creating a theatrical work of art as was *Pietas victrix*, and such art was also capable of appealing to all the emotional demands of the audience.

Very important to the embodiment of the allegorical elements in baroque drama was *the ballet*. In the period of High Baroque, it was no longer sufficient merely to insert a dance in a scene; far more now, as is the case with *Pietas victrix*, dances are inherent to the main action. The casting calls specifically for thirty-three performers to compose a *"Chorus Romanae Juventutis et saltorum."* Throughout the work song and dance are frequently intertwined. In *Pietas victrix* another twenty-two performers are required for a *"chori musici."* Choruses, ballets, and vocal solos are to receive musical accompaniment in order to create the artistic synthesis. For the training of instrumentalists among the stu-

---

[6] Nicolaus Avancini, *Pietas victrix*, incl. 9 scenes (Wien: 1659, owned by the Osterreichischen Nationalbibliothek); cit. in Kindermann, *op. cit.*, 457-460.

dents, many Jesuit colleges in southern Europe had added their own *"Seminarium musicum"* to the curriculum. Many of the then popular oratorios were produced in such seminaries, as, for example, were the works of the talented P. von Oer, which were composed at the Hildesheim Gymnasium, and which called for complete settings suitable for musical dramas.[7]

As a dramatic vehicle, High Baroque operatic pieces could make wide use of the *stock charac-ter.* A very consistent alternating of serious scenes with comical ones correlated very well with the contrapuntal rhythm of High Baroque art generally, as well as with the shifting play of scenes having shallow and deep staging. Bidermann, in his *Cenodoxus,* might well have developed his character-izations—the flatterer, the lazy servant-thief who sells the victim's own rug to him—from Roman com-edy. Avancini, however, seems well aware of the baroque folk-comedy being performed on the conti-nental stages of the wandering actors. He seems to have an even better acquaintance with the comedies of Gryphius. The latter's comical situations and interludes were elevated to strong contrasts in the serious and comical scenes, and arranged in a sequential pattern of devastating and exalting scenes.

[7] Kindermann, *op. cit.,* 459.

Figure 31A.   Scenes from *Pietas Victrix,* Performed at the University of Vienna Aula Theatre, 1659. Hell scene: Satan in a cart pulled by dragons. cf. Figure 31B. Attack on the fortress of Maxentius. Kindermann, *op. cit.*

Having discussed some of the basic elements important to production in the High Baroque theatre, one may pass to a consideration of the show in its Act sequence. What experiences might an audience anticipate from a presentation of *Pietas victrix?*

In *Pietas victrix,* as mentioned, the Christian Emperor Constantine conquers the heroic warriors of Maxentius. The struggle, set with impressive antithesis according to the contrasting dream appearances of the two leaders, proceeds at times with elaborate, extended public scenes, at other times with a striking magician entrance, then again with land and sea battles. While Emperor Constantine dreams that the apostolic guardians of Rome, Peter and Paul, appear to him with promise of victory, the tyrant Maxentius dreams that he is visited by the ghost of Pharaoh, who has commanded him to oppose the people of the Lord. A warning angel rises out of a column of fire. One spectral appearance follows another in succession. The force of evil appears in the person of Demas, the magician. At the close of Act One, allegorical appearances—Piety, Impiety, Victory, Industriousness, and Admonition—unite in chorus to impress the ending emphatically on the eyes of the viewers. During the dream sequences, the Tiber River turns red, flying serpents and furies appear, fire breaks out, the earth quakes, Cerberus howls from hell, a dragon spews fire from its concealed throat, and a threatening blare of horns fills the whole region.[8]

[8] Nicolaus Avancini, *Pietas victrix,* Prologue and Act I; complete text in Willi Flemming's *Das Ordensdrama, Deutsche Literatur,* Reihe Barock, Barockdrama, Bd. 2 (Leipzig: Verlag von Philipp Reclam, 1930), 184-303.

Figure 32A. Scenes from *Pietas Victrix,* 1659. Neptune on the Tiber with sea-horses, tritons, and mermaids, cf. Figure 32B. Flight of the magician Demas to Hain. Kindermann, *op. cit.*

While the choruses, thoroughly operatic, accompany the battle between Piety and Impiety, the scene moves to a high pitch of intensity through the air war of the eagle against the dragon, the dragon fighting for Impiety and the eagle fighting for Piety. When the setting of the battle shifts to the tent scene of the opposing forces, the war appears to extend beyond mere earthly realms. Hell-born demons appear in the heavens in order to plunge the hosts of God into confusion. Act Two has reached its climax. The beginning of Act Three is played in hell (Figure 31). Satan comes onto the stage riding a dragon cart. It concludes with the magician Demas being carried through the sky (Figure 32B). In the Fourth Act, flames leap from the water. Subsequently, an attack is made on the fortress of Maxentius, the warriors of Constantine making a living staircase of themselves to surmount the city walls (Figure 31B). On the Tiber, Neptune appears with sea-horses, tritons, and mermaids (Figure 32A). But as the scenes move to a sea battle, with the frames at stage right showing ships and those of stage left the city walls, the script states that the fleet of Crispus fought against the city.[9] Here, also, heavenly hosts are ready with assistance, a victory which Avancini achieves through the vertical emphases of High Baroque scenic art.

[9] *Ibid,* Act IV, Scene 9, 279: *"Crispus urbem classe oppugnat."*

The victory thus accomplished, a fugue style chorus is introduced to conclude the show. Triumph-al arias of *Victoria* and *Pietas* are interwoven with duets between *Consilium* and *Industria,* these again being periodically interrupted by *Fama prima* and *Fama secunda.* The duet of *Consilium* and *Industria* proclaims the victory of Pietas to the Orient and the Occident; the duet of *Fama prima* and *Fama secunda* proclaims the victory to earth and heaven. Joyfully, the whole chorus takes up the song of *Pietas,*

Vicit Pietas, Deus at toto

Orbe triumphat. [10]

The illustration of the *Scena Ultima* (Figure 33) indicates the manner in which the glory chorus of a *Ludi Caesarei* could be made to appear on the stage. Emperor Constantine is seated on a victor's throne, placed before a majestic triumphal arch. He is surrounded by his underlings. Before Constantine is his son, Constantine II, who is called as the successor to the throne of his father. From the clouds a host of angels offers its blessing. But on top of the tripartite arch which sweeps over the throne arises the double-eagle of the Habsburg House, so that the ultimate goal of the historical struggle may be evident to everyone in the audience. [11]

---

[10] *Ibid.,* Act V, Scena Ultima; cit. in W. Flemming, *op. cit.,* 299-303.

Vocal interludes were not particularly new in the Jesuit theatre by 1659, and ballet intermezzi had been established as an expected routine since a Munich performance of *Samson* in 1586, when well trained children danced as nocturnal birds. In *Gottfried von Bouillon,* 1596, the production called for a dance of the spirits ascending from their graves.[12] How the graves were designated is not explained. But with the dynamic theatre art of the High Baroque, the dance became integrated with the whole production to compose a lively, picturesque argument set to music. The Early Baroque "scena muta" of the Jesuit theatre was transformed into danced scenes. The instrumental music suggested many new alterations in the older format. The main work of composing, however, was carried on in Vienna, where Italian opera and church music were by no means at odds with each other. All the songs, choral pieces, dances, and musical interludes were for the most part composed by the court choir director. A conjecture by analogy would lead one to expect that the court also had available talent to use at its discretion for assisting in the work of stage decoration and costuming, and that the designing work would become the responsibility of the court architect. It is, then, not at all unlikely that the more

[11] *Ibid.;* cit. in Kindermann, 457.

[12] Kindermann, *op. cit.,* 457.

Figure 33. *Pietas Victrix,* 1659. Concluding scene with Emperor Constantine seated on a throne, flanked on either side by soldier ensembles. Constantine II, his son and successor, stands before the throne. A double eagle rises in flight from the arch behind the throne. C. Niessen, *Das Bühnenbild.*

important decorations for *Pietas victrix came from the hand of Giovanni Burnacini,* and that these designs had been submitted with the first draft for the show, completed before the death of Giovanni Burnacini in 1655.[13]

In addition to the significant performance of *Pietas victrix,* which established Nicolaus Avancini and his University Aula shows as a leading example of Viennese High Baroque theatre then being offered to the general public, some mention may also be made of the martyr dramas and allegorical pieces. These were also given for the entertainment and edification of the general public.

The martyr dramas of the High Baroque Jesuit stages, given in the German speaking sections of southern Europe, frequently were elaborated into lavishly decorative sacrifice scenes, in which large groups of priests enacted heathen customs. The final effect usually consisted of a martyr's prayer, delivered by a woman, which caused the pictures of heathen deities to be destroyed by a lightning bolt from God.[14] Triumphal trains, elegant victory banquets, and huge glory scenes with festive dance accompaniments were part of the necessary equipment for Jesuitical performances in the High Baroque period. Crownings, wedding celebrations, and pompous high-level consultations were just as important to the scenic appeal as were the cloud revelations, visions, oaths of the dead or of ghostly apparitions, and magical and demoniacal effects.

Allegorical pieces, as already noted for *Pietas victrix,* were likewise a regular part of shows in the second half of the seventeenth century. In the performance of *Constans in aula religio,* given at Hildesheim in 1664, each of the five Acts is introduced by a special allegorical *Praeludium musicum.* Rivers, countries, and continents are likewise personified in glory scenes.[15] Although the allegorical embodiment of some central tendency in the action often related to a star actor, a matter of no small consequence to the performing arts of that time, the descriptive details which the author felt were necessary for the stars extended to 1120 pages, if he followed some of the authoritative and frequently re-edited compendiums of the time.[16]

---

[13] *Ibid.,* 458.
[14] *Ibid.,* 458.
[15] *Ibid.,* 458.
[16] *Ibid.,* 459.

6

The Burnacini Style

A. GIOVANNI BURNACINI

While theatre of the High Baroque was blossoming for public admiration and education at the Viennese University Aula under the direction of the philosophy and rhetoric professor, Nicolaus Avancini, the more refined elegance of the court productions became the responsibility of Giovanni Burnacini.

Prior to his immigration and fame at Vienna, Giovanni was employed at a public theatre in Venice, called the Teatro SS. Giovanni e Paolo (Figure 34). Since pictorial records of the thriving theatre life in Venice are very few, there is inadequate information concerning the decors of the Venetian designers during the period of 1630 - 1645. Bjurström, emphasizing a view which I also share, states that this absence of data may be attributed to the function served by the Venetian theatres; "it was a public entertainment and not part of a prince's plans to further his political or cultural status."[1] Giovanni Burnacini is commonly thought to have lived and to have begun his career at Mantua; but these points have never been established. Some recent information has altered the earlier conclusions of Biach-Schiffmann that nothing is known of Giovanni Burnacini before his connection with the Theatre of the Apostles and his entry in a scenery contest about 1644.[2] *Le Pretensioni del Tebro e del Po,* a dramatic piece given at Ferrara in 1642, indicates that Giovanni Burnacini was in that town to build a theatre for a staged tournament, as required by the performance.[3] An engraving dedicated to L. T. Pira shows that Burnacini was also in Venice during the same year to help design the Feast of the Virgin

---

[1] Per Bjurström, *Giacomo Torelli* (Stockholm: Almquist and Wiksell, 1961), 46.

[2] Flora Biach-Schiffman, *op. cit.,* 1 - 15; Bjurström, *op. cit.,* 46: "Biach-Schiffmann is very incomplete in her treatment of Burnacini's work in Venice."

[3] Introduction by Antonio Pio di Savoia. Illustrated with four engravings (Repr. by F. Torrefranco, *Il primo scenografo del popolo,* G. Burnacini, *Scenario,* 3 (1934), 191, 193 - 194. Cit. in Bjurström, *op. cit.,* 45.

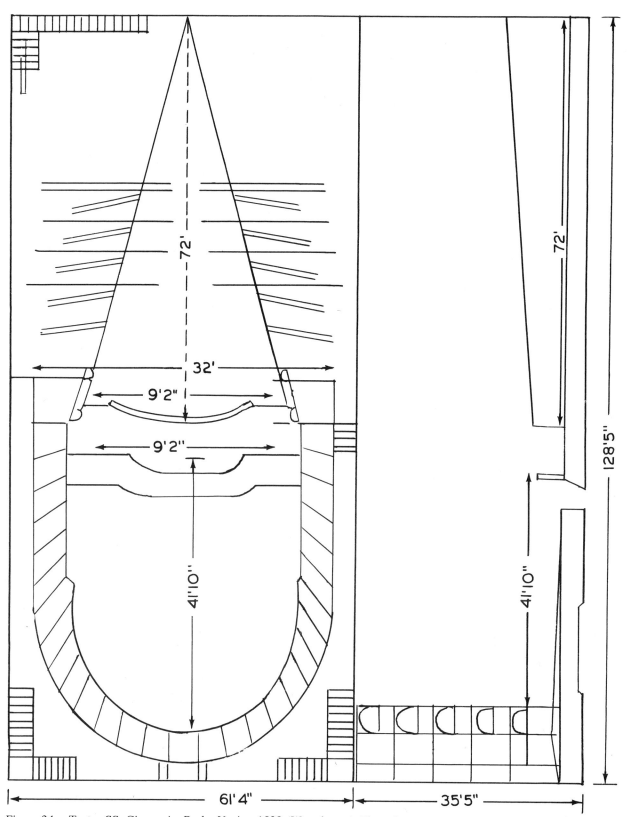

Figure 34.   Teatro SS. Giovanni e Paolo, Venice, 1639 (Worsthorne). Floorplan.

Figure 35.   The first Vienna Opera House of Giovanni Burnacini with the tournament scene from *La Gara,* 1652. Kindermann, *op. cit.*

Mary at St. Mark's Square.[4] So far as is now ascertained, the first known stage work from Giovanni Burnacini was the setting for *La Finta savia* at SS. Giovanni e Paolo in 1643. But a text passage accompanying the libretto of this opera implies that Burnacini may also have been the principal designer for other operas given at SS. Giovanni e Paolo since 1641. This would include *Le Nozze d'Enea con Lavinia* (1641), *Narciso ed Eco immortalati, Gli amori di Giasone e d'Isifile,* and Monteverdi's *L'Incoronazione di Poppea* (1642), for the passage states "Le machine, e le scene con numerose mutationi sono state inventate dal vivacissimo Signor Gio. Burnacini da Cesena, il quale fù gli anni adietro il primo, che ravivò i Teatri di Venetia con questa maestrosa apparenza."[5] About 1644, Giovanni Burnacini placed second to Giacomo Torelli in a design and staging competition at Venice. The designs submitted by Torelli were those for *La Finta Pazza,* which established him as a scene designer of international repute.[6] Giovanni Burnacini again received favorable public attention in 1650 with his setting for *Bradamante,* and once more in 1651 for his work on *Gl'Amori di Alessandro magno e di*

Engraving dated 30/8 dedicated to L. T. Pira; cit. in Bjurstrom, *op. cit.,* 45.

G. Strozzi, *La Finta savia* (Venezia: 1643), 184; cit. in Bjur-

ström, *op. cit.,* 45.

[6] Biach-Schiffmann, *op. cit.,* 9-10.

Rossane, performed at the Teatro SS. Giovanni e Paolo. Following these productions, he accepted a commission to be the court architect at Vienna, where he remained until his death in 1655.[7]

As a precedent for understanding the stage and theatre of the Caesarea Corte, the Teatro SS. Giovanni e Paolo at Venice is significant. Worsthorne has interpreted the dimensions and floor-plan as follows:

Over-all length	128 ft. 5 in.
Over-all breadth	61 ft. 4 in.
Height	35 ft. 5 in. (from floor to ceiling in auditorium)
Stage depth	72 ft.
Width at the proscenium arch	32 ft.
Length of auditorium	41 ft. 10 in.
Breadth of the centre boxes	5 ft. 7 in.
Breadth of the rest of boxes	4 ft. 6 in.
Width of the corridor ceiling boxes	3 ft. 7 in.
Width of the orchestra pit	9 ft. 2 in.
Length of the orchestra pit	4 ft. 7 in.
Width between orchestra and pit	5 ft. 7 in.

Unfortunately, Worsthorne has provided neither the original measurements nor a metric interpretation of the same.[8] Consequently, no attempt has been made either in the table or the accompanying floor plan to re-interpret the feet and inches into the metric system. The reader, however, may draw his own implications by comparing the Giovanni e Paolo floor plan of Figure 34 with others provided in this text.

A sloping ceiling at the theatre was not only a functional covering; it provided a fine acoustical construction above the fore-stage. Staircases at the rear of the stage could facilitate the work of the stagehands in operating complex machinery.

Emperor Ferdinand III had become convinced in 1651 that the time was ripe for the construction of a theatre "in Corte Cesarea" to honor the birth of the Spanish Infantin Margarita. The building was completed during 1651, and in January, 1652, *La Gara* (The Contest) was successfully performed in Giovanni Burnacini's new theatre (Figure 35). The plot of that opera calls for a tournament among the four powers of the earth, with Jupiter rendering the decision through *Honor,* the highest virtue, to *Europa,* played by the emperor.

The building which housed *La Gara,* as illustrated in Figure 35, contained a two-tiered gallery and auditorium, which was supported by rounded arches and columns, decorated by eagles. In line with the recommendations of Johannes Kepler, concave, metal eagle-reflectors could produce a really

[7] Bjurström, *op. cit.,* 45-46. "The attributions are based upon a passage in Burnacini's preface to H. A. Cicognin, *Gl'amori di Alessandro magno e di Rossane,* Venezia 1651, p. 8. 'A me dunque, che per i diletti dell'Architettura, e di macchine posso con verità dirmi il primo, quanto al tempo c'habbia ornate scene ò fatte macchine in quest Città, l'ultima delle quali è stata la Caduta di Bellerofonte nel T. di S. Giovanni e Paolo, a me dico è toccato di porre sul mio, benche picciolo Theatro, un Alessandro grande.' It is clear from G. Salvioli . . . that 'La Caduta

di Bellerfonte' was part of *Bradamante* by P. P. Bissari, which was indeed the last opera produced at the Teatro SS. Giovanni e Paolo before *Alessandro.* Cf. Torre-franco, . . . *Enciclopedia dello spettacolo,* 2, Roma 1954, col. 1373-74 (E. Povoledo) who consider *La Caduta di Bellerofonte* as an otherwise unknown opera from 1641 . . . "

[8] Worsthorne, *op. cit.,* 30-31, incl. floor plan.

fine lighting effect. The main structure was of wood. The areas suggested for the parterre and orchestra, however, do not permit of any conclusion in regard to their architectural relationships with the stage and auditorium, although they would appear to be similar to those in the floor plan of the Teatro Giovanni e Paolo. The perspective, assumed from upstage, locates the "duke's seat" of the emperor in the center-front of the auditorium, the seat being decorated by a canopy supported by two sculptured figures on pedestals. The auditorium could have been lighted from fixtures attached to the mounted eagles on the columns, but whether such fixtures were ever installed is not recorded. The Cesarea Corte, as this theatre came to be known, was renovated for performances periodically until its destruction during the Turkish invasion of 1683.[9]

The stage area of the Cesarea Corte is something of an enigma, since no measurements have been recorded. Yet the stage had to be large enough to accommodate frame staging with *changement à vue* technique, probably with the assistance of machinery in an understage section; but, again, this is only conjecture based on knowledge and experience available to Giovanni Burnacini from his work at the Teatro Giovanni e Paolo in Venice. Whether an inner stage existed at the Cesarea Corte is also not certain, but the stage had to be deep enough to house about five sets of frames as well as the flying equipment required in the fifth act of *La Gara*.

An analysis of the requirements pictured for Acts III and V of *La Gara* implies the following production items:

a. The composition and picturization to be supplied in Act III is that of a cosmopolitan tournament, with the actors being stationed and moved to areas of the stage most appropriately designed to facilitate their recognition as Europe, Asia, Africa, and America. The dominant position, of course, is ultimately Ferdinand's appearance on the forestage, personifying Europe.

b. The costuming necessary is that of renaissance and knightly style with plumed hats. Properties are lances, spears, torches, and musical instruments appropriate to a festive tournament.

c. The *dramatis personae* are those of the nobility.

d. The stage lighting is not altogether evident, but performances were commonly held in the late afternoon, when a few lamps might prove sufficient to light the stage and set it in contrast to the darker auditorium. In the illustration, torch bearing pages are stationed at stage right and stage left, and the effect of this lighting is indicated by the shadows of the combatants in the centre of the stage. For lighting the auditorium, fixtures could have been set in the mounted eagles of the auditorium columns, but there is no evidence to show this.

e. Music was provided by an orchestra in the pit. Additional music to embellish the scene, as well as to cover prop and machinery noise, was played on stage by flutists and drummers, located downstage from the torch-bearing pages.

The foregoing account refers to the scene depicted for Act III. In Act V, above-stage machinery is brought into the performance as Jupiter enters, flying on an eagle in order to render a decision on the tournament. Presumably, the remaining set would be similar to that of Act III. Other unique elements which climax the opera in Act V are as follows:

[9] Kindermann, *op. cit.*, 491.

    a. A character bearing the symbol of *Honor* approaches *Jupiter,* descending from above-stage onto stage-centre, and accepts from him a prop signifying the victory-palm. *Honor* must then rush the victory-palm downstage to *Europa,* danced by Ferdinand III.

    b. *Europa* (Ferdinand III) accepts the victory-palm and subsequently receives the gratitude and obeisance of all the other participants in the contest, who recognize him as their conqueror.

The significance of *La Gara* in the evolution of Viennese opera life was at least two-fold: 1. The designs and staging tecniques, including *changement à vue,* which were used by Giovanni Burnacini, began a new current in the evolution of spacious Viennese Baroque opera; 2. The education of the public in concepts of authoritative power and political consolidation received its first imperially sanctioned operatic form through these magnificently embellished baroque designs.[10]

The Fasching celebrations of 1652 which had begun so pleasantly led to a long chain of theatrical festivities, so that in almost every alley new scenes could be observed, some being enacted with Turkish costumes, some with Moorish costumes, and others of a similar style. In this same context, the Empress requested the performance of a *Daphne* opera to highlight the February celebrations, quite probably the *Daphne* of Rinuccini.[11] The main action of the opera seemed to concern Daphne's being transformed into a laurel tree, while the court musicians played in majestic and well conducted accompaniment. Among the most charming of spectacles to be seen was the swift flight of Mercury streaking here and there in the sky and through the theatre, as if he were lightning itself. Again, following the transformation of Daphne into a tree, twelve ladies of the nobility led by their Empress crept from beneath the earth and from individual trees to dance an immeasurably beautiful ballet.[12]

The following year Giovanni Burnacini, together with his son Ludovico, constructed another two-gallery theatre at Regensburg, next to the Cappuziner Cloister, for the pleasure and education of the powerful German princes attending Ferdinand's conference.[13] In order to demonstrate the power of this new art for political instruction, *L'inganno d'amore* was performed at the Regensburg Theatre in February, 1653, with text by Benedetto Ferraris and music by Bertoli. The third member of the creative trio, Giovanni Burnacini, was responsible for the designs, staging, and machinery. As depicted in Figure 23A, the design suggests a conservative, linear approach to staging, with some effort at increasing spatial dimensions for the better unification of scenery and action. Similar to the departure of Longhena's Venetian architecture from the Manneristic style of Palladio, the line emphasis falls on vertical and diagonal dimensions, coupled with rounded arches and rounded columns. The first four Palladian columns in the center of the stage seem to have been planned as set pieces, enabling the dancers to perform within the set. In keeping with the spirit of Palladian style, the detailed set includes highly elevated and sculptured pedestals with bust-decorated entrances; but the back-shutter and the accompanying impression of a three-dimensional statue change the entire set style into the baroque architectural mood set by Baldassare Longhena in Venice after 1630. The costumes are very similar to those used in *La Gara,* and they may well have been the same, especially if the ac-

---

[10] *Ibid.,* 491.

[11] *Theatrum Europaeum,* Bd. VII, 175; cit. by Kindermann, *op. cit.,* 491-492. The conjecture is based on the popularity of Rinuccini's opera, the improbability that a less significant work would have been selected for the occasion, and the brief time-interval (2-3 weeks) for writing, composing, and designing a new *Daphne* opera comparable to that of Rinuccini.

[12] *Ibid* ". . . Mercurius, bald hie, bald dort in der Luft so eylends

fortgefahren und das Theatrum durchflogen, als wenn es der Blitz gewesen wäre; wie denn auch, nachdem die Daphne in den Baum verwandelt worden, zwölf der Kaiserin Hof-Damen, ein jede aus einen Baum, und also gleichsam aus der Erden hervor gekrochen kommen, welche Ihrer Kays. May. einen über die massen schönen Ballet getanzt."

[13] cf. 34-35, 41-42 for data on the construction of the theatre.

tors of the previous performance were dancing again. Renaissance designs, military breastplates, spear and lance properties, and plumed hats predominate in the illustrated sixth scene of *L'inganno d'amore*.

Following this last publicly acclaimed work of his career,[14] Giovanni Burnacini was succeeded in office at his death by his son, Ludovico Ottavio Burnacini. During the brief period the father had lived and worked for the Imperial Court in Vienna, a strong tradition of High Baroque staging had established itself. This tradition included:

1. A unity of artistic enterprise in musical composition, libretto, and staging.
2. The construction of two-gallery theatres with proscenium arch joined to the auditorium and provision made for frame-staging with *changement à vue* by means of under-stage equipment, which Giovanni Burnacini developed contemporaneously with his competitor, Giacomo Torelli.
3. The effort to resolve problems of aesthetic space so as to unify scenery and movement, the dancers being allowed to perform within the scenery. Entrances are placed to the right and left, behind the proscenium.
4. A lengthened stage of between 20-24m is used to accommodate above-stage flying and glory machines, which were housed behind the shutter dividing the fore- and inner-stages.
5. Experiments with special lighting effects and with lighting contrast between the stage and the auditorium, intensified through the interplay of convex and concave surfaces, were a keen interest with Giovanni Burnacini.
6. Sloped auditorium ceiling; renaissance staging; Palladian arches and columns; and baroque architectural styling, which shared Longhena's emphasis on concave surfaces and diagonal dimensions.

B. LUDOVICO BURNACINI

Ludovico Ottavio Baron Burnacini rose to prominence in theatre architecture rather slowly, inconspicuously, but decisively. At age fifteen, Ludovico arrived in Vienna with his father to assist in the construction of the new Cesarea Corte Theatre (1652). During the following year, he continued as an apprentice to his father for the building of the Regensburg Theatre.[15] His understanding of the latter structure would seem to have been a valuable asset to him in carrying out the emperor's commission for the engineering of two theatres which were to be ready for the 1661 Fasching celebrations.

While only nineteen years old, Ludovico inherited the mantle of chief engineer, or architect, at the Imperial Court from his father, Giovanni Burnacini. Unfortunately, he did not inherit a salary equal to that of his father, as he complained in a letter to Emperor Ferdinand III.[16] He also inherited his father's Judenplatz house, for which Ludovico had not sufficient funds to pay the taxes, and the position of family leadership, without an adequate income to support the family. Nor did these circumstances undergo significant improvement for some ten years, until the wedding festivities of Leopold I in 1666-67, when Ludovico was fully reinstated at the income level of his father.

A further problem to the aspiring young architect was the death of Ferdinand III in 1657. Dur-

[14] cf. 35.

[15] cf. 34-35, 41-42, 70, 136.

[16] Biach-Schiffmann, *op. cit.*, 41-44.

ing his short term under Ferdinand III, Ludovico Burnacini received only one major assignment, that of designing the opera *Teti* in 1656.[17] *Re Gelidoro,* performed in 1659, has not been ascribed to Burnacini and may have been the work of Giovanni B. Angelini, whom Leopold I had sought to use as a replacement for Burnacini. No other work of Angelini has come to light.

Leopold I had his attention focused anew on Ludovico Burnacini when works of the designer were accepted for a performance of *Il Pelope geloso* in Venice, 1659.[18] Consequent upon that production Burnacini was rehired as chief architect at the Imperial Court to replace Angelini who resigned at the end of 1658. Although the financial conditions under which the twenty-three year old Ludovico labored for some eight years were not the most encouraging one could imagine, he remained faithful to his vocational status. In all, he remained in the service of the emperor about forty-eight years without interruption. Evidence of this uninterrupted service between 1671-1707 is primarily the excellent recording entered in the theatre account book by the court inspector, Giovanni Benaglia.[19] When he died, Burnacini had long since escaped the days of his poverty and risen to a position of considerable affluence, counting two houses and a vineyard among his many valuable possessions.

During the time he was working on the *Theater auf der Cortina* (1666-1668), Burnacini's salary was established at 1800 Gulden annually, three times that of his father. Encouraged by his progress and good fortune, Burnacini married. But twice he was widowed; and he married for the third and last time in 1680. Through a combination of circumstances, but especially that of his second marriage, Ludovico came into possession of a house with gold columns at the Judenplatz. Although the growing affluence of Burnacini received a severe reversal during the Turkish siege of 1683, his salary of 1800 Gulden annually resumed following the defeat of the Turks. In response to a plea for recompense, Emperor Leopold I granted Burnacini 5000 Gulden in 1700 for the loss of property and possessions during the Turkish siege, when Ludovico was in Italy.[20]

On December 12, 1707, Ludovico Burnacini died, probably of pneumonia, in his home at the Judenplatz. According to his written will, the architect of Leopold's spectacular court operas was buried without pomp in St. Michael's Church.[21] His estate, which went to his widow, included gold, silver, jewelry, wine, paintings, books, weapons, clothing, furniture, and two houses: one in town at the Judenplatz and one with a vineyard, located at Kritzendorf. The law also permitted him to will his annual salary and pension to his widow. Emperor Josef I, who had succeeded Leopold I in 1705, also sent presents and condolences to the widow of Burnacini.[22]

Taking account of Ludovico Burnacini's life work, one finds that it extends to a great variety of activities, encompassing theatre architecture, designs for operas and oratorios, costuming, designs and decorations for festivals, altars and memorial structures, triumphal monuments, interior decorations for the court salons, and construction at country estates owned by the Imperial Court. When one realizes that the actual number of operas which Ludovico Burnacini designed exceeded 115, the designs which have been preserved are comparatively few, leaving much uncertainty to the serious student of theatre history.

[17] cf. 75; Hadamowsky, *op. cit.,* 71: Sept. 13, In the castle for the birthday of the emperor. *Theti* (drama set to music) 5 Acts, libretto by D. Gabrielli; music by Bertali; scenery by Burnacini (6 settings), ballet by Ventura (3 designs), machines by Burnacini (15 technical arrangements). Italian text by Matteo Cosmerovio, 26 pages; cit. in *Theatrum Europaeum,* VII, 868, and Alexander von Weilen, *Zur Wiener Theatergeschichte.*

[18] Bjurström, op. cit., 265.

[19] cf. 37.

[20] Biach-Schiffmann, *op. cit.,* 44-46.

[21] Alexander Hajdecki, *Sammlung* II, Convolut IV, Handschriftenabteilund der Nationalbibliothek Wien, A-F, Testamentskopien; cit. Biach-Schiffman, *op. cit.,* 46. Totenregister 11669: "Am December 12, Ludwig Octavius Baron Burnacini, 71 Jahre. Kays. Mundschenk in seiner behausung am Judenplatz an der Lungensucht."

[22] *Ibid.,* 46-47.

On the basis of these designs, however, four periods may reasonably be conjectured for the designing work of Ludovico Burnacini.[23]

A. 1652-1659. During this period the work of Ludovico dovetails with that of his father, Giovanni, and the designs of Ludovico after 1655 mostly elaborate the methods and motifs of Giovanni.

B. 1659-1667. This period indicates greater independence, with the development of significantly more complex stage machinery, having larger dimensions and a richer use of mass, line, and color.

C. 1667-1680. Beginning with the production of *Il pomo d'oro,* the activity during this period is marked by intensified brilliance and fantasy, which reaches its peak of artistic development in *Il Fuoco Eterno Custodito delle Vestali* at the *Theater auf der Cortina,* 1674.

D. 1680-1707. An apparent lack of artistic unity during this period may be due less to discouragement and old age, as suggested by Biach-Schiffmann, than to the large influx of new information and the extensive experimentation with newer concepts. In addition to sketches on war and pestilence, experiments are made with lighting for night shows at the Favorita.

Attempting to distinguish these periods of development by orientation on the machinery inventions of Torelli, Biach-Schiffmann was led to assume that the designs from 1652-1659 implied no mechanized *changement à vue,* whereas those of Ludovico Burnacini after 1659 clearly indicate the influence of Torelli.[24] The penetrating research of Worsthorne and Bjurström on Venetian opera houses and designers between 1639 and 1655 has left this hypothesis in a very questionable status.[25] The hypothesis is further complicated by the acknowledgment that the productions of 1659-1660, performed at the Tummelplatz Theatre, virtually required the inventions usually ascribed to Torelli. The studies of Franz Hadamowsky and the pictorial comparison by Heinz Kindermann[26] imply that these performances were not in a new stage-house, as argued by Biach-Schiffmann, but in a reconstructed and, to be sure, richly re-decorated building which father and son had set up originally in Regensburg. Certainly the redecoration would indicate a growing independence of Ludovico Burnacini in his work.

The opera, *La forza della fortuna,* from which the second period of Burnacini is dated, concerns a complex intrigue among the lovers in the story, Queen Irene of Athens and her two rival suitors, King Thearchos of Crete and King Orontes of Armenia. The plot had been handled before, especially in the mid-seventeenth century as designed by Grimaldi Bolognese in *Trionfo della Pietà,* given at Rome, in 1658. Ferdinand Tacca also handled it for Cavelli's *Hypermestra* at the Teatro della Pergola in Firenze, in 1658.[27] But the designs of Burnacini represent an effort to surpass these earlier shows by a greater complexity of painting and movement, combined with a richer detail of architectural embellishment.

In the one illustration selected from this opera (Figure 36), the stage of the reconstructed Tummelplatz Theatre is planned to house a cliff scene, with cliff frames at stage left embellished by trees. The suggested setting implies the use of five frames at either side of the stage and an illusionary per-

---

[23] *Ibid.,* 47. This periodization differs somewhat from that of Biach-Schiffman, the conjectures being derived from the addition of data by R. Meyer, H. Kindermann, and F. Hadamowsky.

[24] *Ibid.,* 48.

[25] cf. 29-30, 65-68.

[26] cf. 41-42, Figures 23A and 23B as correlated by H. Kindermann.

[27] Biach-Schiffman, *op. cit.,* 51; *Enciclopedia Dello Spettacolo.* I, Tav. III.

Figure 36.   Cliff and seacoast scene from *La Forza della fortuna e della virtu* by Teofilo, music by G. Tiberti and scenery by L. Burnacini; Vienna, Theatre of Corte (sic!), 1661. *Enciclopedia Spettacolo,* I, Tav. III. No final evidence now exists for the location of the performance; performance at the Tummelplatz is assumed on the basis of design correlations and a newspaper note from *Frankfurter Relations;* a quite lovely comedy, in which a great variety of theatrical scene changes were particularly pleasing to watch ("eine überaus schöne Comoedi . . . worrinnen die vielfältige mutations theatri absonderlich wol zu observiren waren.") Hadamowsky, *op. cit.,* 72.

spective painted on a back shutter. The back shutter is meant to display a seascape, so that the audience receives the impression that all of the forestage action is occurring on the rugged seacoast. The total artistic effect is accomplished by lessening the emphasis on the painted frames while putting greater stress on the diagonal composition expressed in the costuming, action and use of properties, which include swords, lances, shields, and flags.

A subsequent production, *La Zenobia di Radamisto* (1662), which Biach-Schiffmann ascribes to Ludovico Burnacini, is not so verified in Franz Hadamowsky's tabulation of performances. The show was recorded for the Hofburg and may have been that of a Venetian troupe for whom the theatre account books record a payment.[28]

The third period in the creative development of Ludovico Burnacini is one of extraordinary elegance. Since the unusual synthesis of artistic creativity during these years merits a more detailed treatment, influential as it also was for the foundation of peculiarly German Baroque theatre and opera in Central Europe, a further discussion of this period is left to the next chapter. There attention will be directed to the most widely known work of Viennese High Baroque Opera, *Il pomo d'oro,* giving special consideration to problems of staging. The designs for this festive opera are there examined for the support and emphasis they lend to the innovations and motifs of this period.

[28] *Ibid.,* 51; cf. F. Hadamowsky, op. cit., 72. No other performance was recorded at that time for the Tummelplatz Theatre; but *La Zenobia* cannot now be assigned with certainty to the Tummelplatz Theatre.

Some indication of the Burnacini creativity during these years may, in general, be gathered from two other notable shows: *Il Ratto delle Sabine* and *La Monarchia latina trionfante.* The former opera, given in 1674 at the Cortina, lasted for two days. This division, according to the preface of the opera book, was made in order not to weary his majesty excessively during the warm time of the year. The story concerns the plight of the Sabines and their rescue by Apollo and his court. The opening scenes, suggest the use of deep staging, including the use of an inner stage, in order to alternate interior and exterior settings. For interiors, the shutters and forestage would be used; for exteriors, Burnacini had extended the inner stage to a back shutter. The interior requires only five painted frames and a painted shutter after the fifth wing to compose a castle scene with high, straight walls adjoining a garden in perspective. As in the seacoast setting of *La Forza della fortuna,* imposing grandeur suggested by height, together with comforting peace suggested this time by the distance perspective of a garden, is presented in marked contrast to the choreography of the dancers, whose movements and costumes employ diagonals most emphatically. The restless activity of baroque culture, utilizing the El Greco arch motif and stress on diagonal dimensions, is intended to evoke the excited attention of the audience. The costumes, in the tradition of Giovanni Burnacini, are expressive of renaissance ideals, with one Roman soldier possessing a long, flowing cape.

In the concluding scene, which is not here illustrated, a glory machine is required to transport Apollo in a carriage, surrounded by four deities and twenty-four angelic beings — twelve on either side to represent the hours and division of the day — from above stage onto the main stage. The machine, a cloud-masked device used in *Il pomo d'oro* in 1668, probably operated from the inner stage, since a separate flying device carrying Daphne into the foreground before Apollo would appear between the third and fourth wings. Symbolically enough, the twelve hours are to carry sand glasses on their heads.[29]

The festival opera, *La Monarchia latina trionfante,* was apparently the last major work for which Vienna was famous prior to the Turkish invasion, although several colorful performances had attracted audiences to the open air shows at Laxenburg. This opera has been thought by some to be the most fanciful of the compositions, displaying a unique quality of beauty and grandiloquence.[30] The text description runs as follows: The *Earth* accuses the enemy powers of *Indolence, Ambition, Tyranny, Hate* and *Confusion* before the throne of *Jupiter.* The gods decide to investigate the age of mankind and to have the most peaceful government restored to prominence. *Saturn* summons the four great world monarchies to appear, and *Discord* involves them in a battle, to which the gods are also parties. The rulers are Minos, Darius, Alexander the Great, and Caesar, the last of whom is victorious. The Roman Empire is restored to prominence, and Leopold I is celebrated as its newly acclaimed representative. As illustrated in Figure 37A, a stage curtain was used to separate the actors from the audience prior to the opening of the show. The curtain had probably been used in earlier performances.[31] Correlating with the prologue, the design indicates that a charming idea had occured to the opera creators: *Happiness,* costumed as a pilgrim, steps forward to address the audience; then he swings up the skillfully decorated curtain while he is himself carried off into flight at stage left. Behind the curtain, half raised, an immense landscape is visible, filled with ensembles of nobility, foot soldiers, and horse-men, to which are added elephants and camels.

---

[29] Biach-Schiffmann, *op. cit.,* 58.

[30] *Ibid.,* 59.

[31] *Ibid.,* 59.

Figure 37A. *La Monarchia latina trionfante:* Curtain and opening scene. cf. Figure 37B: Salon of the Asträa. Discord in a cloud casts lightning toward the main stage.

Following an underworld interior setting in the second Act, the Scene shifts, as illustrated in Figure 37B, to the exterior for an elegant salon of the *Asträa* "Prächtiger Saal der Asträa"). In the full spirit of the High Baroque culture, the series of frames have serpentine twistings, in whose winding lines three human forms are respectively set. The Scene is the victory of a hero over two of his opponents who bow before him. The opponent farthest downstage center holds the head of a corpse, the remains of which lie upstage. Above the center stage *Discord* rides in a cloud machine and casts flashes of lightning toward the earth setting. Orchestral drums could be used to simulate thunder and the lightning flashes could be traditionally accomplished with the aid of a bowl containing powdered sulphur and a candle. Lightning bolts since Serlio "demanded the drawing of a thin wire over part of the stage; down this might be run a rocket covered with gold foil." (A. Nicoll)[32] While the goddesses of justice astride the frames of the forestage confirm the victory of the House of Habsburg over its foes, *Discord* in the cloud machine, wielding her lightning flashes, brings conflict among the four world powers. The baroque frame designs extend from the forestage to the shutter area, where a huge set piece with

[32] Sebastiano Serlio, *Treatise on Architecture,* transl. in Allardyce Nicoll, *Stuart Masques and the Renaissance Stage* (New York: Benjamin Blom, Inc., 1963), 137; Barnard Hewitt, *The Renaissance Stage* (Coral Gábles, Florida: University of Miami Press), 35.

steps joins the forestage wings to a decorated colonnade. This could have been raised to a considerable height *(c.4-5m)*. As always with Ludovico Burnacini, the detailed figures at the top of the columns are subordinated to the concept of axial perspective. The colonnade setting would have been admirably suited to the deep inner stage of the Theatre auf der Cortina. Costuming is again in the renaissance tradition for both men and women. The crowned goddesses, seated on top of the wings hold swords and balance scales in the right and left hands, respectively.

In addition to the staging techniques at the Cortina, indicated by the illustrated analyses just presented, Ludovico Burnacini earned acclaim throughout Europe for his decorations of open-air shows, especially at Laxenburg and at the Favorita.[33] These performances were most significant during the last, experimental years of his life. While the method of scene changing for these shows remains unknown, and it appears unlikely that an understage area existed at Laxenburg, the Favorita, and other outdoor locations to house scene change machinery; the deep staging which Burnacini retained, as shown in Figures 28 and 29, probably required many stage hands to move the frames on and off stage in the pre-Torelli fashion.

Other examples of the Burnacini creativity which are probably from the post-war era have been

---

[33] cf. 48-50, where an attempt has been made to analyze two scenes from separate shows at the Favorita pond.

identified by Joseph Gregor and are given here as Figures 38 and 39. The first design is a caricature of the ravages and destruction caused by war; the second, a perspective design of a destroyed city, presumably ruins resulting from military conflict. It is not known that these designs were ever realized on the stage or even so intended. Yet the huge stone structures and baroque curves employed in the caricature are motifs unmistakably similar to those which decorated the curtain for *La Monarchia latina trionfante,* even though the theme for the opera is given a different treatment (Figure 37A). Staging techniques for an interior hell scene are used in the caricature; and with the use of frames, flying machines for the devils and their victims, a few set pieces utilizing wheels and a pole, and props made from tubes and vases, together with a mechanical turtle, a person would be well on his way to reconstructing the design for realization on the stage. Some damp, smoking straw and fireworks would help complete the fun.

The illustration of the destroyed city was a common feature in Burnacini designs. Often such a picture would be used to help decorate a backdrop or a back shutter, as was the case with the hell scene of *Il pomo d'oro.* Certain characteristics set this design apart from all other destroyed city paintings, however. In this design the contrasting arches and intersecting diagonals convey a mood of triumph and hope against the depressing ruins created by the Turkish siege, although in many respects the work represents a return to the geometrical patterns of the Teatro Olympico at Vicenza (1584). Again, in this design common people with common dress are included, busily carrying lumber for the

Figure 38.   Hell, a caricature on the ravages of war and famine, by L. O. Burnacini.

Figure 39.   A destroyed city, sketched by L. O. Burnacini.

reconstruction of the town. One is repairing his cart at downstage right, while the two townsmen in the center could be discussing the future layout of the buildings. All characters, including two women at center left, wear the contemporary costumes of their vocations for the period of 1700. It is a vigorous expression of the faith that Austrian High Baroque culture and art has been basically the creation of the Viennese populace. While the scene depicts a quite realistic view of the destruction wrought by war, this view remains within the total aesthetic spatial and perspective context of baroque art, where the repetition of the curved arch motif is stated in a manner that encourages a mood of spiritual hope, and ascendance.

By way of restatement, the development and contributions of Ludovico Burnacini to the art of stage design may be given as follows:

A. 1659 - 1667. This period of relative conservatism, when he was achieving the mastery of his architecture and engineering trade, has the following marks:
1. rectangular scenic sections with distance perspective;
2. comparatively shallow forestage designing, using five wings and a back shutter;
3. construction of an understage area (Regensburg and Tummelplatz) for use of machinery to facilitate the *changement à vue* manner of scene changing;
4. absence of designs for inner, deep staging.

B. 1667 - 1680. This period of artistic synthesis is especially characterized by the following developments:
    1. introduction of an inner stage at the Cortina, creating a practicable three-part stage with deep perspective;
    2. combination of fore and middle stages;[34]
    3. orchestra pit is continuous with the forestage;
    4. unification of space through scenery, movement, and machinery which could be operated from the inner stage;
    5. intensified fantasy in stage décor, heightened by a brilliance in the use of colors;
    6. a manner of subordinating choral direction (Chorregie) in favor of more complete architectural effect, an effect which is not evident in the designs from his earlier period.
C. 1680 - 1707. Most of this period, coming after the Turkish siege and expulsion from Vienna in 1683, may be characterized as follows:
    1. experiments with realistic picturization of contemporary scenes—city destroyed, utilizing contemporary costuming and set pieces, although the scene may never have been realized in actual theatre production;
    2. experiments with breaking up and moving the axial perspective—Min. 29 5fa. of the *Pestepidemie,* which shows a suggested extension of a wing at downstage right to approximately two-thirds of the stage width;[35]
    3. experiments with constructivist designing, as indicated in the *Pestepidemie,* showing a two-story building inclusive of compartments and functional doors. The pestilence, as a historical event, occurred in 1679;
    4. satirical caricature of war, using baroque, serpentine curves and extreme distortion of figures and properties;
    5. development of illuminated night shows at the Favorita pond and grottoes, employing pipe-lights.

Summary

The foregoing conclusions will be treated further in the next chapter, which concerns a detailed analysis by Acts of *Il pomo d'oro.*

Himself a pupil of the Jesuits, Leopold I cultivated the new art of the opera assiduously for the religious and political orientation of all his subjects. The political orientation seems usually to have outshone the religious themes. Throughout this chapter an effort has been made to show the unique contributions of three outstanding theatre designers who gave forceful direction to the theatre culture and education at Vienna during the second half of the seventeenth century. The flowering of operatic performances by Nicolaus Avancini at the University Aula gave significant media for training univer-

---

[34] cf. 29 for the interpretation of Hans Tintelnot and H. Kindermann.

[35] Min. 29 5fa., pencil sketch 230 370 in the Nationalbibliothek at Vienna; cit. as illustration 56 in Biach-Schiffmann, *op. cit.*

sity students in the preservation of the Latin language and Roman Catholic symbolism. As value orientation for praise and obedience to the new Caesar, Leopold I, they were even better, tending to subordinate the Church to the Habsburg State. The new direction provided by High Baroque culture and theatre at the University of Vienna found stronger reinforcement at the Imperial Court, where the Jesuits Sbarra and Draghi supplied libretti for the elegant settings of Giovanni and Ludovico Burnacini. By no means the least among the composers of music for these spectacles in honor of the emperor, who was to restore peace and political consolidation in the heart of Europe, was Leopold himself. The dynamic synthesis of High Baroque culture, for which Leopold I earnestly sought to educate his subjects, was at least attained on the stage by the technical advances of Giovanni Burnacini and the artistic synthesis accomplished through deep staging techniques of his even greater son, Ludovico Burnacini. The *avant garde* stage décor by this leader of the post-Torelli generation in Europe asserted its claim to prominence with the production of *Il pomo d'oro,* to which attention now turns.

7

Il Pomo D'Oro

Introduction

Among the festive operas of the seventeenth century, *Il pomo d'oro* has been accorded a prominent position. The fame of its performance continued to fill the pages of theatre notes many decades following the first performance. Forty years afterward, one historian could still speak of the opera as the most elegant one ever seen. The enthusiasm of this Austrian historian, Rinck, is not to be wondered at, even though his exaggeration that *Il pomo d'oro* was given three times weekly for a whole year before freely admitted public audiences has no basis in existing evidence. Current Austrian scholarship further supports the judgment of G. Adler that such a concept is highly improbable.[1] Whether the opera was performed elsewhere in Austria or the Holy Roman Empire is also a matter of conjecture. Rinck credited the opera with a hundred performances; nothing is now definitely known on this matter, however. It seems unlikely that the opera was ever revived after the death of Margaretha, for whom the climactic scenes were created, on March 12, 1673.

When the text of *Il pomo d'oro* was printed for public sale and circulation, the librettist, Francesco Sbarra, S. J., wrote in his preface that he earnestly desired his readers had rather been viewers of the

---

[1] Rinck, *Leopold des Grossen Leben und Thaten I* (Cölln, 2nd ed., 1713), 157; cit. by G. Adler, *Denkmäler der Tonkunst in Österreich,* Jahrg. III/2-Bd.6 (Graz: Akädemische Druck-und Verlagsanstalt, 1896, 1959) Einleitung v.; cf. Biach-Schiffmann, *op. cit.,* 53 and H. Tintelnot, *op. cit.,* 57, who reiterate Rinck's assertion; F. Hadamoswky, *op. cit.,* 36-37, shares the view of Adler supported here. H. Kindermann, *op. cit.,* is silent on the subject.

original production. Other than the designs provided for the text by Ludovico Burnacini, wrote Sbarra, the reader would find only the poetry of the librettist, which without all the valuable décor used to present it upon the stage remained but a skeleton of inadequacy from the pen of its author. He, Sbarra, could complain even more, since he found himself unable to depict fully and completely for the reader the exquisiteness of the music, the beauty of the building, the superiority of the scenery, the richness of the costumes, the number of the sets, the variety of the machines, the unusual elegance of the tournaments, the changing patterns of the dances, the boldness of the dueling, the military precision of the siege and defense of the fortress, together with other artistic marvels, which for the most part cover the lapses in the poetry. In all, this *Teatrale festegiamento* might be considered to have exceeded all previous works for elegance and nobility, concluded Sbarra, a matter which the reader might well understand when he realizes that the emperor spared neither time nor money for the production. The entire management had been well supported with the most generous supplies of both.[2]

Concerning the cost of the production, Rinck may not have grossly exaggerated when he estimated it at 100,000 Reichsthaler for the theatre and the production. In round figures of contemporary life in the United States, such a cost would be the equivalent of more than a million dollars, which is not at all unusual for the construction and use of a very important public building. If one calculates further the real estate and labor differentials which have accumulated during the past three-hundred years, the cost in 1970 would, of course, be much greater.

The central ideal of *Il pomo d'oro* is that wisdom, personified in a wise and honorable emperor, is the highest virtue. The theme might be summarized in the following manner: The promotion of any high virtue, though disturbing in its unilateral effects, is wise and honorable; but the greatest wisdom is that which establishes in the person of a holy emperor the unification and harmony of the highest virtues throughout the Christian Empire. Leopold I was not one to overlook the political education of his aristocratic underlings. Regardless of other dramatic shortcomings, the grand court operas of Leopold I were sure to have a unifying concept for political orientation.

In the matter of plot, the shortcomings were certainly evident. The new art form had not yet learned to develop its plot from a conflict implied within the story; consequently, Discord, who exists as a separate entity and hostile force astride a fire breathing dragon, dislikes the musical harmony of the heavenly spheres enough to intrude at a banquet and cast a golden apple among the deities. The apple bears an inscription, "To the Most Beautiful." Conflict enters from outside the original Scenes.

Juno, Pallas, and Venus subsequently dispute among themselves for the title of "The Most Beautiful." To resolve the quarrel, Jupiter chooses Paris, son of Priam, to make the decision among the goddesses because of his perseverance and faithfulness in a distant land. Paris, the audience learns, is in love with Ennone, a beautiful nymph-daughter of the River Xanthes. Incidentally, Ennone also has some affection for the sailor, Aurindo. Mercury, the heavenly messenger, brings Paris the report of Jupiter's plan. Concerned over the involvement of Paris with the disputes of the deities, Ennone becomes depressed; but he reassures her of his constancy. In the succeeding Scenes, the goddesses present themselves before Paris with various promises to persuade him to decide in favor of their respective superiorities. Venus promises Paris the beautiful Helena, Queen of Sparta. He yields to Venus, thus betraying Ennone, and goes off to his rendezvous with Helena.

Juno and Pallas, fearing complete loss to Venus, seek immediate revenge on Paris; Juno requests Aeolus, god of the winds, to have Paris drowned by shipwreck. As a second plan of battle, Pallas re-

---

[2] G. Adler, *op. cit.,* Einleitung vii - ix.

quests Cecrops, king of Athens, to pursue Paris with military arms. Venus, learning of the plot from Cupid, decides to outflank the others by soliciting the allegiance of Mars, god of war, to help the lovers. Paris manages to survive the winds and the military pursuit, and success seems assured when Cupid reports to the triumphal train that the fortress of Mars is under attack by the Athenians.

At a high point in the destruction of the fortress, Jupiter appears to retrieve the apple, which has been hidden in a fortress tower. He promises to please all parties concerned, including the goddesses, in that he will award the apple to the noblest person on earth, who will unite in wisdom all the highest virtues of beauty, honor, and love. The personification of wisdom is Margaretha, who has chosen to rule with Leopold I. Discord and the dragon never re-enter the action after the initial toss.

Typical of the early seventeenth century operas, the events are external to any real development of the plot. The main attraction is the scenery and the action of the characters which, together with musical accompaniment, provide a very loosely knit artistic unity. Sbarra might well complain that without the scenic embellishments of Ludovico Burnacini his libretto was but a skeleton of inadequacy from the pen of its author. Yet, it was this kind of artistic context which offered the aesthetic foundations on which Händel, Glück, and Mozart were to construct their later, monumental operatic works. The scenic innovations achieved in the High Baroque period also permitted the creative artists of the following century a greater expenditure of energy on the development of drama, music, and libretto suitable to the staging concepts which evolved between 1650 and 1720.

When one attempts to analyze the High Baroque operas of the Imperial Court at Vienna, certain difficulties are inevitably encountered. Often the original text is incomplete or non-existent, and no clear evidence is available to demonstrate that the sets were realized in exactly the same manner as is shown in the designs of Ludovico Burnacini. Furthermore, the designs themselves do not always give an unmistakeable impression concerning the use of shallow and deep staging. The designs, however, do offer primary evidence of the intentions of Burnacini for realizing the scenes on the stage. The text for *Il pomo d'oro* is complete, but the music is missing for Acts 3 and 5.

Following the tradition of renaissance staging, the scenes may be expected to alternate in the use of shallow and deep staging. In fact, this method of alternating shallow and deep sets works very well for most of the first three Acts in *Il pomo d'oro*. The prologue begins with deep staging technique, but Act I opens on a shallow stage. The set with which Act I opens is retained for three Scenes, after which an alternate set for Scenes four and five makes use of the deep, inner stage. On the other hand, the alternation of sets within the Acts does not permit the inference that alternation of sets also occurs between the Acts. For example, the apparently shallow set of Act I, Scene 15, seems to be followed by the shallow set of Act II, Scene 1. In the case of *Il pomo d'oro*, the alternation of sets also bears no necessary relationship to their being either exteriors or interiors. An additional problem of interest with this opera is the possibility that all the Scenes of Acts IV and V could have been played on the deep stage of the Cortina. The extravagant settings for the descents, triumphal march, fortress siege, villa of Paris, piazza of Mars with palace in deep perspective, and concluding glory Scene could scarcely be accomplished otherwise.

The musical accompaniment, which has been analyzed in depth by Guido Adler, is worthy of note here. Although the compositions of this opera, written by M. Cesti and Schmelzer, frequently serve little more purpose than the masking of otherwise noisy flying scenes, requiring the use of heavy stage machinery, or the excuse for a soloist to demonstrate the range of his vocal prowess, they are significant in other ways. Somewhat independently of the opera settings and action, sonatas of merit were composed to introduce each respective Act, as well as the prologue. The merits of these compositions have been detailed by Adler and are not further relevant here in the emphasis on stage production. Nevertheless, an additional matter of interest is that Schmelzer, who aided Cesti, represents the first major contribution of a German artist to the development of opera.

The performance Requirements of Il pomo d'oro.

Material Requirements

To return to the production of *Il pomo d'oro,* one might outline the performance requirements as follows:

Number of Acts	5, in addition to prologue.
Number of settings	23, with some repeated for separate Scenes in the same Act; e.g., II, 1-5 again in II, 8-9.
Order of Sets:	
Prologue	Area of Austrian Fame
Act I, 1-3	The Kingdom of Pluto
Act I, 4-5	The Kingdom of Jupiter
Act I, 6-10	Forest Landscape on Mount Ida
Act I, 11-14	Palace Courtyard of Paris
Act I, 15	Garden of Joy
Act II, 1-5; 5-8	Seaport
Act II, 6-7	Entrance to Hell
Act II, 8-9	Seaport (of II, 1-5)
Act II, 10-12	Armed Camp of the Athenians
Act II, 13-14	Tritonian Swamp
Act III, 1-2	Underworld Cave of Aeolus
Act III, 3-5	Valley Landscape with Xanthos River
Act III, 6	Armory of Mars
Act III, 7-10	Sea during a Storm
Act III, 11-12	Amphitheatre
Act IV, 1-2	Pleasure Garden of Cedars
Act IV, 3-5	Temple of Pallas in Athens
Act IV, 6-9	Heaven with the Milky Way and Region of Fire
Act IV, 10-13	Forecourt to the Palace of Venus
Act IV, 14-15	Fortress of Mars
Act V, 1-8	Villa of Paris
Act V, 9	Piazza of Mars
Act V, 10-11	Heaven, Earth and Sea
Number of interiors	7 (3 shallow, 4 deep)

Number of exteriors	16 (7 shallow, 9 deep)
Number of main characters:	12, as follows,

Jupiter
Juno
Pallas
Venus
Mars
Priam
Ennone
Paris
Aurindo
Filaura
Cupid
Momus, the jester

Number of important minor roles: 20, as follows,

Gloria Austriaca
Discord
Pluto
Prosperina
Mercury
Charon
Furies (3)
Aeolus
Winds (4)
Neptune
Adrasto, a general
Alceste, a general
Eufrosine, one of the Graces
Cecrops, a general
Victory

Additional entrances are supplied in the conclusion as Jupiter presents the golden apple to Margaretha, who together with Emperor Leopold, leads the entire company in a climactic ballet.

Choruses and dances are intermittently required, such as:

Prologue dance
Ballet led by Pluto and Prosperina
Deity chorus for the banquet Scene and glory Scene
Nymphs to accompany Ennone
Supporting chorus for Juno in her gallery
Sailors chorus
Tritons chorus
Mermaids chorus

Priest chorus
Soldiers chorus
Choral ensembles for the siege and defense Scene

On-stage technical operators are also required for managing a fire-breathing dragon, two elephants, two lions, and a turtle.

In summary, about 150 characterizations and costumes are needed for 73 regular performers, 4 machine operators, a 32 person chorus, and 41 extras to be used in the battle ensembles of IV, 14-15. Acts II, 10-12, and IV, 3-5, suggest the use of a real dog and a real sheep.

The successive Scenes, analyzed for production purposes, may be explained in the following manner.

Production Analysis
PROLOGUE

Plate I

According to the German preface, the remainder of the text being in Italian, the audience should witness appearing art structures, flights and the like in the Prologue. Use of the deep stage is required. Gloria Austriaca, mounted on the flying Pegasus, sweeps from the rear of the inner stage across the entire performance area, the Teatro della Gloria Austriaca, which is decorated with trophies and equestrian statues bearing Leopold I and 12 lesser rulers of the Holy Roman Empire. The entrance is revealed from between opening clouds.

Setting. —As this design would be realized on the stage of the *Theater auf der Cortina,* three staging areas would be utilized: forestage, middle stage, and inner stage. The design suggests the use of two five-wing sets on the *forestage,* a slightly extended shutter on the *middle stage* which is arched over from either side by cherubs (probably cut-outs) holding a wreath, and a closed shutter in painted perspective on the *inner stage.* A single *set piece,* supporting a horse on which Leopold I is mounted, could be either three dimensional or a two dimensional cut-out and appears on the middle stage directly behind the shutter opening. The *cloud* behind Pegasus is in all probability not a painted perspective; its repetition with variations for all the Acts and Scenes clearly indicates that it is a masked machine, ready for use in deity and glory revelations. In summary, the prologue design presents all the main staging elements which were employed at the Cortina and which were to be used throughout the performance of *Il pomo d'oro:*

    I. Three staging areas;
    II. Symmetrical setting with deep perspective;
    III. Five sets of wings on either side of the main stage;
    IV. Middle stage with shutter; also adequate space for large entrance and exit groups. The middle stage is also convenient for set pieces erected by a technical crew.
    V. Individual flying apparatuses operated from positions between the middle stage and rear wall of the inner stage.
    VI. A large cloud machine above the inner stage.
    VII. Shutter at the farthest extent of the inner stage.

Costume. —The costuming is that which was typical renaissance dress for men and women in the theatres of Venice during the sixteenth and seventeenth centuries.[3] The women wear long, embroidered dresses, sometimes with a sash; the men, breast plates and plumed headdress. A royal Moor at stage left symbolizes the power of Spain.

The Prologue concludes as Cupid and Hymen fly heavenward, making humorous gestures to each other. The machines for these flights are also suggested in the design presented.

ACT I

Plate II

Setting. —Scenes 1 - 3 are suggested by the design, but the Scene presented is the climactic one for Scene 3. Throughout the Scenes, shallow staging is used with only four of the five forestage wings being shown. A partially open shutter behind the fifth wing is extended toward the center of the stage

---

[3] Millia Davenport, *The Book of Costume,* I (New York: Crown Publishers, 1948), 288 - 289; II, 491 - 495.

from either side. A second shutter, decorated with a concave unit (drop), closes off the inner stage; but enough space is available to accommodate a flying machine, which Burnacini usually shows as appearing above stage, between the third and fourth wings.

Action.—Scene one, not shown, introduces a ballet by Pluto and Prosperina, who lead the spirits and demons of the underworld. The entire action occurs within the kingdom of Pluto, elegantly depicted on the wings and shutter through High Baroque twisting, color, and fantasy. The ballet and songs continue through Scene two and into Scene three, when the conclusion of the ballet is marked by the sudden appearance of Discord astride a fire-breathing dragon. This startling entrance having already accomplished its purpose for the Scene and the audience, Discord quickly exits without singing another comment.

Mechanical effect.—The flying dragon could have been a wood cut-out, large enough to mask the machine and seat on which Discord sits. Discord probably feigns holding the dragon rein, while he actually could be operating a bellows on burning wet straw in order to produce smoke from the mouth of the dragon.

Costume.—The costuming of the spirits is similar to that of the Prologue, but the demons would seem to require hairy skirts and masks in a medieval tradition, together with claws on the toes. Their wing attachment might be from stiff cloth. Realistic tails help to complete the impression (A. Nicoll, *Masks, Mimes and Miracles,* 189-191).

Lighting.—The lighting effects necessary for contrast and intensification of effect could come from fire pots which are more evident in later Scenes.

Plate III

Setting. — Scenes 4-5 are accomplished with the use of deep staging technique, prepared during the previous, alternate shallow setting. Once again the wings on the forestage are changed. The shutter after the fifth wing is partially extended, but a cloud ground row and a low wall have been introduced, extending the width of the stage, and perhaps serving to mask the supporting mechanism used for the banquet of the gods. A reasonable conjecture, based on the arrangement in the design, might be that the large cloud machine, usually reserved for above-stage revelations, is in a stationary position on the floor of the inner stage to provide the needed positions of a banquet Scene. The ceiling of clouds might be achieved by borders and leg drops.

Action. — At the close of the deity banquet, Discord once more appears, this time on a cloud between the third and fourth wings, stage right, and announces her intention to cast the golden apple to the gods at the banquet. The apple is cast, and the beautiful harmony exhibited in the preceding song, ballet, and scenic display is violently disturbed. Although a thunder machine could have intensified the sensational effect, no indication is given for the employment of such a device at this place in the text. The use of lighting and sound effects is usually given a clear indication by Ludovico Burnacini.

Costume. — The costuming of the preceding Scenes in renaissance, Venetian style is continued, but the special dress effects for Scenes 4-5 are indicated by the satyrs on the forestage. Allowing some freedom for artistic idealization, the satyr effect could approximate realization through the use of genuine goat skins, readily available in Austria, and the employment of foot mounts. The symmetrical balance of the setting is completed in deep perspective by the painted shutter used on the inner stage, behind the banquet Scene.

Plate IV

Setting. — Scenes 6 - 10 alternate back to shallow staging, with the combined use of the fore- and middle stages. A shutter after the fifth wing closes off the inner stage, while the disuse of the inner stage for this setting is further indicated by the closed cloud machine, suspended above the inner stage area.

Action. — At the beginning of Scene six, the audience is presented with a ballet and songs, performed by Ennone and her nymphs in a woodland setting. Baroque motifs are retained through the twisted lines of the tree trunks and branches. Again, in the climactic eighth Scene depicted by the design of Burnacini, the dance is interrupted by the flight and descent of Mercury to earth. He reports the plan of Jupiter to Ennone and, as indicated in the text, returns once more to heaven. Scenes 9 - 10 return to a completion of the ballet, but on a sadder note since Ennone now fears the loss of her lover.

Mechanical effect. — The machine which brings Mercury to earth is possibly the same machine used to transport Discord in Scenes three and five. The machine again appears above stage right, between the third and fourth forestage wings.

Costume. — The Venetian Renaissance costuming of Ennone and her nymphs is complemented by the equally traditional dress of Paris and the shepherds, although the shepherds may be expected to have a somewhat less elaborate dress than does Paris. Special costuming effect is reserved here for Mercury, who wears a flowing cape, winged sandals, winged hat, and carries his winged, serpentine staff as a prop. Other properties include shepherd staffs.

Plate V

Setting. — Scenes 11 - 14 alternate to the deep setting which Ludovico Burnacini depicts for Scene 14. All of the elements introduced by the Prologue are once more given full play: five wings, partially opened shutter after the fifth wing, closed shutter with painted perspective at the farthest extent of the inner stage, flying apparatuses coming from the right and left stage areas, between the third and fourth wings, and the descent of the large cloud machine, operated from the inner stage area. The light and dark areas illustrated for the inner stage suggest that no inner stage wings were employed in the Scene, but that the major portion of the inner stage was left clear to accommodate the descent of the large cloud machine.

Action. — As Scene eleven opens, two flying angels carry Momus, the court jester, on their wings to earth. Both angels return to heaven (cf. Prologue).

The entire setting is in the palace courtyard of Paris, where Paris, of course, is leading a ballet supported by six dancers. The musical dialogue of Paris and Momus continues for two Scenes. In Scene 13, however, the luxurious golden gallery of Juno descends from heaven. With Scene 14, the climax is heightened by a setting in which the effects of the preceding entrances, Momus and Juno, are embellished by the appearance of Pallas, sitting in her Gate of Honor as she descends to Paris with tempting songs of weapon strength and symbols of victory.

Costume. — A main variation from previous costuming which seems to appear in this Scene is that the courtly participants in the ballet are recommended to complete their Renaissance dress with ego-elevating wigs of the High Baroque period.

The most significant property is the sword of Pallas.

Special effects. — The scenic effects created by the flying machines could probably be realized by cloud masking and the use of cut-outs. A concave unit may again have been used for Juno's gallery.

A special lighting effect, as oil lamps overhead and mirrors in the gallery, might intensify the golden effect. But this is not certain.

Plate VI

Setting. — Scene 15. When the set is alternated[4] for the appearance of Venus to Paris, the natural return is made to shallow staging with the inner stage closed off by the second shutter. The clouds of the sky indicate that the flying machines operated from the middle- and inner stage areas are not now being employed. This design may have omitted the front wings on the forestage, but a possibil-

[4] cf. 85, 91-93.

ity also exists that only four wing sets were used. The architectural effect at stage center might have been most conveniently achieved by the use of a partially open shutter painted in perspective.

The use of shadows by Ludovico Burnacini suggests that the fountain, located at upstage center on the forestage, was an independent set piece, either two dimensional or three dimensional. As no evidence is now available to show how the *Il pomo d'oro* designs were realized on the stage of the Cortina, it is not possible to ascertain whether or not real water was used for the fountain piece. The whole set piece may be a painted design. Tradition favored this interpretation. On the other hand, several mechanical devices known to Da Vinci, Galileo, and the contemporaries of Burnacini could have made the fountain at least partially realistic; e.g., vacuum valves, pressure valves, and novel variations of the Archimedean screw were all part of seventeenth century technology. If Leopold I wanted a realistic fountain, a fountain complete with flowing water would have been on the stage.

Action. — The Scene, which marks the conclusion of Act I, takes place in the Garden of Joy, where Venus, accompanied by a chorus of Beauty (five girls) and a chorus of six little servants of Cupid, tempts Paris to decide in her favor with promises of love. Momus stands downstage left of Venus. She succeeds, and Act I ends with Venus leading Paris off to a rendezvous with Helena, Queen of Sparta.

Costume. — The extra costuming required for this Scene would be that of dressing additional Cupid figures, wearing diapers and wings and carrying arrow containers. Bow and arrow props must be provided for each Cupid. Since the chorus sings, the little figures are real and would have been drawn from court and town families. They might even have been very young members of the chapel and local church choirs.

ACT II

Plate VII

Setting. — The opening Scenes, 1-5, of this Act continue the use of the shallow stage with five wings on either side of the forestage, depicting cliffs, shrubbery, and ancient ruins from which trees are growing. The painted perspective shutter at the middle stage shows boats, lighthouses, and seascape to complete the impression of a seaport.

The staging at this point is by comparison quite simple, requiring no use of set pieces, ground rows, or flying machines.

Action. — The entire five Scenes are concerned with a romantic ballet and songs by Paris and Ennone, supported by ensembles of nymphs and sailors. A variation is offered by Filaura, who expresses her desire for the love of Aurindo. Aurindo, who is not in the Scenes, is apparently still in love with Ennone.

Costume. — The sailors of Paris, being employees of a court, are all pictured as wearing wigs in the seventeenth century style. The vocation of the sailors is symbolized by their possession of harpoon props.

Plate VIII

Setting. — Scenes 6-7 of Act II are set in hell. Deep staging is used together with an unusual manipulation of wings and possibly drops to create a brilliant red and fiery hell-mouth. From the elements of the design, the first four wings seem to have been omitted. Only the fifth *forestage wing,* rugged and painted in almost impressionistic fashion with tortured looking skulls, is discernible. The main features of the hell-beast, including teeth, ears, and eyes, may be a single cut-out drop (cf. cloud scenery of Act I, 4-5, and the armory pillars of Act III, 6), placed at the shutter line, directly behind the fifth forestage wing. Although the fantasy of Ludovico Burnacini justifiably evokes admiring wonder through this highly theatrical achievement, Horst Richter (*Johann Oswald Harms,* 189) has established that the stagecraft involved had been conventional at the University of Vienna Aula since 1605. A hell-mouth of this proportion would have been familiar to Nicolaus Avancini.

Behind the drop appears a river Scene, which could have been realized either by Sabbatini's roller technique, or by Furttenbach's cut-out waves. In either case, the moving waves effect could be created by connection to an offstage machine. The apparent motion of the boat in the waves, as it goes across

the stage, was a technique known to many stage designers in the seventeenth century. Ropes and rollers, as recommended by Sabbatini, could manage the task without great difficulty.

The dark-light contrast of the design again serves to indicate that the burning city in hell is a painted perspective on an *inner stage* shutter, although inner stage wings could also have been used to create the impression. The contrast of light is commonly used to indicate the shutter against the darker wings.

From all available evidence, real *fire* was probably used quite liberally in this Scene. Bellows operated below the ears could help blow the flames shown at stage right and stage left. Fire pots mounted in the drop could create the impression of fire coming from the nose of the hellbeast. The fire props of the Furies could well be hollowed cylinders, containing wet burning straw.

Action. — As the hell Scene begins, only Charon is seen and heard as he rows his boat, used to transport the Furies and demons from the city of hell across the river Acheron. When he reaches the forestage edge, Scene 7 begins with the Furies — Aletto, Tesifone, and Megera — appearing to rise from where Charon has docked and flying into the world. Each Fury sings a separate song of the woes he is bringing because of the discord among the gods.

Setting. — Scenes 8 - 9 alternate to the shallow stage, and the same set is repeated that was used for the first five Scenes of Act II. At a high point in Scene 9, Venus and Cupid appear on a chariot in the sky, but quickly disappear again. Since the set is shallow, the flight probably required the operation of a machine near the shutter area.

Costume. — The costumes to be used had already been introduced at Act I, Scene 1, Pluto's cave, and Act I, Scene 4, the banquet.

Mechanical effects. — The Furies are expected to be flown on the forestage, beginning from a position near the first shutter line (cf. Act I, Scenes 1 - 10).

Plate IX

Setting. — Scenes 10 - 12 finds the setting once again on the deep stage. The military camp of the Athenians is shown, with Cecrops and Adrast leading a soldiers chorus. The five wings of the forestage depict the tents of the soldiers, who are grouped in two choral ensembles around their leaders on the forestage. Two additional ensembles are probably used in the shutter area, following the fifth forestage wing. The light-dark contrast technique of Burnacini suggests that about four additional wing sets have been introduced on the inner stage before the final shutter concludes the distance perspective. A dog appears to be observing an insect on the forestage, downstage right.

Action. — Following solos by Cecrops and Adrast to the accompaniment of the soldiers chorus, Scene 11 reveals Pallas, sitting in her chariot in the sky. The chariot appears to be drawn by two owls, probably cut-outs connected by reins to the chariot. Pallas carries a lance, emblem of her honor. Throughout Scenes 11 - 12, Pallas solicits the aid of Cecrops against Venus and Paris.

Costume. — The soldiers are dressed in Venetian Renaissance style with traditional breastplates and helmets. The properties include shields and varied weaponry. Adrast carries a token staff of his military leadership. The horses are probably painted on the wings.

Mechanical effect. — The position of the cloud, as well as the structure of it and the size of the chariot, implies that the large inner stage machine, masked with many clouds, is used for the revelation of Pallas in this Scene.

Plate X

Setting. — Scenes 13-14, departing from customary practice, continue the use of the deep stage. The tent wings of the preceding set are changed to wood wings, depicting a forest region surrounding the Tritonian Swamp, birthplace of Pallas. The audience is entertained with a tournament ballet, Amazonian style, presented by the virgins of Athens. At the far right and far left of the forestage stand two soldiers, guards for the tournament. The middle stage area is once more a water scene, but without any required wave motions. Beyond the swamp water, following the fifth wing, is simply a shutter on the inner stage with mountains in painted perspective.

Costume. — No new costume requirements seem to have been introduced. Properties for the scene include shields and lances for the guards and the virgins.

Action. — Scene 14 concludes Act II as Pallas is again revealed on the inner stage cloud machine, but apparently this time without her chariot and owls. Pallas sings in response with the guards.

This setting is repeated in the following Act, Scenes 3-5.

ACT III

Plate XI

Setting.—Scenes 1-2, depicting the subterranean cave of Aeolus, is played on a shallow stage, probably. The cloud machine in which Juno is revealed sitting during the second Act is apparently operated from the shutter area, or near it. The wing set is a relatively simple Burnacini design of huge boulders painted with the Roman arch motif which was so characteristic of High Baroque art. The long halls extending from the main cave seem to be painted shutter perspectives. Although the distance perspective is divided into four parts to allow for greater attention on Aeolus upon his throne, a three dimensional set piece, the Scene remains essentially balanced and symmetrical with a deep axial perspective.

Action.—The action is introduced by the arias of Aeolus and his winds, sung throughout Scene 1. The revelation of Juno begins Scene 2, and her duet with Aeolus is concluded with a flight of the Aeolian winds from the forestage (cf. II, 7) as each in turn—Eurus, Auster, Zeffirus, and Volturnus—makes a musical comment.

Costume.—The winds are noticeably topless dancers, who might have been members of a local church choir. The simple skirt costume below the waist seems simple enough to manage, but special wing attachments held on by shoulder straps complete the effect. As with the demons, these wings also could have been from a stiff cloth. The wind effect shown remains something of a mystery and might only have been the designer's way of indicating the use of a traditional wind machine offstage for acoustical effect.

A rod is provided as a property for Aeolus to symbolize his authority in the subterranean kingdom. The set piece on which he sits is probably a painted, wood structure sufficiently solid to function as a throne.

Plate XII

Setting. —Scenes 3-5 discover the deep stage again in use. The closed clouds above the stage show that the flying machines are not in use for this setting. The wings of the forestage present a forest landscape, guiding the eye of the viewer to the River Xanthos after the fifth wing set. A deep perspective is completed by river falls and shore woods on the inner stage. This result appears to be accomplished by the use of only the first wing on the inner stage, perhaps the first two wings, followed by the perspective view on a shutter.

Action. —As the Scene opens, Aurindo, who is disappointed that Ennone has spurned his love in favor of Paris, announces he is about to end his life by drowning in the river. Momus, the court jester, appears from between the fourth and fifth wings at stage right just in time to rescue Aurindo, who is already taking the fatal plunge.

   Costume.—The costumes are the same ones which were used by these actors in earlier Scenes (I, 6, and I, 11). The design seems to suggest, however, that Momus has on a harlequin mask.

   Special effect.—The water effect could be essentially the same as that used in Act II, Scene 6, and again in Act II, Scene 13.

Plate XIII

   Setting.—With Scene 6, the return is made to shallow staging as the audience is treated to an elegant view of Mars's Armory. The flying machines are in storage where they in fact remain for the rest of the Act. The absence of dancers from within the wings at stage right and stage left makes it difficult to ascertain whether one is looking at separate pillar supports connected to cut-out leg drops, or at total, flat leg drops cleverly painted in perspective to illustrate the shields, weapons, the ammunition of the arsenal. A precedent for separate columns by Ludovico Burnacini and his father has been evidenced in Figure 26, and no reason forbids a similar manner of staging for the Scene of Mars's Armory. The same analogy allows one to conjecture that the ceiling consists of several borders, let down by ropes. The shutter perspective appears to be the same boat scene employed at Act II, Scenes 1-5, but it may be different since the boat prows are not at the same distance as in Act II.

   Action.—The text calls for Venus and Mars to sing a duet as she appeals for and wins his help. This is apparently accomplished on the forestage to the dance accompaniment of servants and soldiers.

Except for one soldier at stage center, between the third and fourth wings, the entire ballet seems to be danced before the scenery.

   Costume.—No new costuming is indicated, and the helmets of the soldiers seem to highlight the opposite, flamboyantly feathered hats of the ladies.

   The shadowing technique of Burnacini further suggests that the set be made more realistic by the introduction of a *small, cut-out cannon* just before the front wing at stage right. The cannon balls farther to the right and left are probably painted on the wings. Real ammunition was obtainable, of course.

Plate XIV

   Setting.—Scenes 7 - 10 alternate to the deep stage in order to depict the onset of a thunderstorm at sea. The wings on the main stage illustrate rocky cliffs, embellished by a few wind-tossed trees on an otherwise desolate seacoast. Appearing at the shutter line seems to be the same water device which was introduced at Act II, Scene 6, only the waves must now be gradually manipulated to greater violence. The large, wood, cut-out ship, which is rolled and rocked behind the artificial waves, must be large enough and have supports to hold a sailor chorus of six men. Beyond the sea, on the deep stage, is again a shutter painted with dark storm clouds. The boat seems to be operated on the inner stage, before the shutter.

Action.—Scene 7 prepares the audience for the coming storm. The rolling of distant thunder becomes louder as the storm increases in intensity. This effect could have been achieved by the mounting roll of drums in the orchestra. Another general theatre tradition was to have a stagehand roll heavy shot down a long wood trough. Lightning effects, possibly set in the large glory machine above the inner stage, could have been made realistic by the use of wired squibs.[5]

Scene 8 is a continuation of Scene 7 and is introduced by the appearance of Venus, being transported on a scallop shell (cf. Figure 3). She is surrounded by mermaids. From the opposite side of the middle stage, Neptune appears riding in a chariot which seems to be pulled by seahorses, probably cut-outs. He is surrounded by Tritons, who convey the impression of swimming between the waves. Together with Paris, who is on the boat, Venus and Neptune sing arias which are accompanied variously by choruses of mermaids, Tritons, and sailors.

Special properties to complete the characterization would be a pitchfork for Neptune and perhaps horns for the Tritons, although the latter are not indicated by either the design or the text. The *costumes* of the mermaids call for fishtail attachments in a traditional renaissance manner.

The *setting for Scenes 9-10* are not clearly designated by Burnacini, but one may assume that, as the storm subsides and the deities make their exits behind the forestage wings, Filaura enters on the forestage to sing a solo amid the cliffs of the seacoast. At the conclusion of her aria, she is discovered by Aurindo. The entire Scene 10 then moves to a romantic close in the duet sung by Aurindo and Filaura.

[5] A. Nicoll, *op. cit.,* 137.

Plate XV

Setting and action. — Returning to the shallow set, Scenes 11 - 12 conclude Act III with two short choral Scenes and a knightly tournament fought on the forestage before an amphitheatre setting. Curved, painted wings, turned diagonally, create a solid, semi-circular effect. They are completed at the end of the forestage by an illusionary entrance, painted on a shutter. The explanation for this new technique was published four years later, 1672, by Troili, to whom credit has often been given for the concept.

Costume. — No new costumes or properties are introduced for these closing Scenes, but the combatants are expected to be equipped with swords and shields appropriate to the tournament.

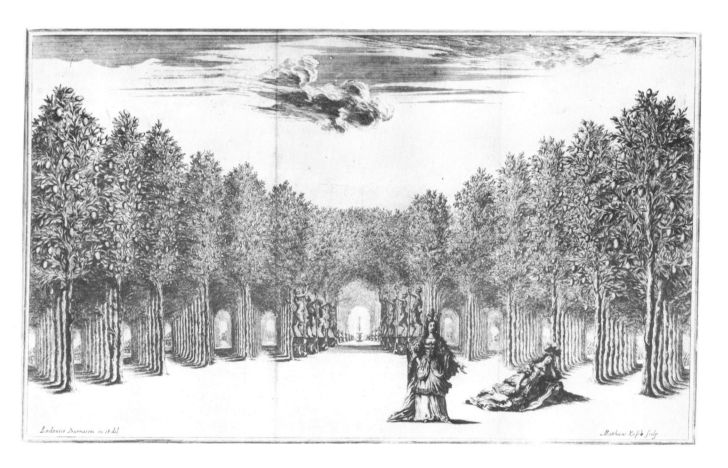

Lodouico Burnacini in et del.   Matthæus Küsel fculp.

ACT IV

Plate XVI

Setting. — Act IV, 1 - 2 take place in a garden forest of cedar trees. Benches, decorated with sculptured Satyrs are painted opposite each other on partially extended shutters. On the second shutter is a perspective painting of a fountain. The cloud above indicates the disuse of the deity machine of the inner stage.

Action. — Throughout Scene 1 Ennone wanders about the forest and benches, singing an aria which expresses her fear of lost love. The aria concluded, she sleeps (left forestage). Filaura enters as Scene 2 begins, and she comments in solo on the sleeping Ennone, who eventually is wakened by the voice of Filaura, as shown in the Burnacini design. A duet by the two girls completes the action of the Scene.

Costume. — The costumes remain the same as in preceding Scenes.

Plate XVII

Setting. — Act IV, 3 - 5 depict the Temple of Pallas in Athens with the five front wings on either side of the forestage turned diagonally, creating the illusion of a solid wall with columns and statues (III, 11). The scenery standing on the stage could indicate either shallow or deep staging technique. While the alternation of scenes, requiring a deep set for the next scene, favors a shallow technique, the light-dark shading, which Burnacini otherwise uses to specify shutters and wings, favors a deep technique. Certainly the climactic action occurs on a deep stage.

Before the shutter line is a three dimensional altar which supports a two dimensional picture of Pallas, at least such would seem to be a reasonable conjecture from the fact that the text calls for the picture to fall during Scene 3.

Action. — At the beginning of Scene 3, only the priest chorus and the sheep are on stage at upstage left. While singing a hymn to Pallas, they begin a pagan ritual worship. Properties on the floor to aid the ceremony seem to be a bundle of sticks and a smoking pot, possibly containing hot coals and wet straw. A terrifying earthquake, probably effected by drummers toward the end of the first Scene, signals the entry of soldiers as the picture of Pallas is precipitated onto the stage floor and a middle curtain, a shutter at the middle of the inner stage, appears to rend.

With this startling preparation, the audience is entertained in Scene 4 by a revelation of Pallas with her shield and sword, sitting in the large cloud above the inner stage area. As with Plate XXI, all the elements are in the design, but not in the sequence required by the text of Cesti. While she sings her aria, Adrasto and Alceste with their soldier chorus and dog, who had entered downstage right just prior to the calamity, join antiphonally with the priests in choral responses to the aria of Pallas.

Costume. — Special costuming requires the use of priestly robes and turbans.

Action. — As Scene 5 begins, all characters leave the stage except Alceste, whose solo completes the action for this setting.

Plate XVIII

Setting. — Act IV, 6 - 9 entertain the audience with a *changement à vue* to a representation of heaven with the Milkyway and the Region of Fire. The Region of Fire drop, which follows the fifth wing and is, therefore, on the middle stage, may be a series of borders. They conceivably could be moved (fluttered) from side to side or vertically to simulate fire. No evidence is available to support this hypothesis, however. From this point on, only the impressive deep staging potential of the Cortina is displayed to the audience.

Action. — As Scene 6 begins, Venus is in her star, seated in the deity machine above the inner stage. She sings a solo. The sea motif is returned following the fifth wing set. Wings on the forestage continue the concept of the fire region, using basically cliff wings similar to those of Act III, 7 - 10. In Scene 7, illustrated by Burnacini, Cupid descends from heaven to the sea in a fiery chariot. He is blindfolded and carries his bow and arrow. At the beginning of Scene 8, Juno must appear in a star-covered chariot, approaching the others through the Milkyway. During the concluding scene for this set, Scene 9, two salamanders spanning a fiery chariot must be revealed above stage. Although the entrance of Juno may be reasonably conjectured as made from the right of the inner stage, the implementation of this entrance as well as that of the salamanders remains uncertain. From the fact that this sensational setting utilized a stage-effect which was already a favorite in the British theatres of the Elizabethan period,[6] one may nevertheless assume that the method of staging was rather conventional among the production artists of Burnacini's time.

Costume and special effects. — While no costuming innovations are foreseen for this setting, the special effects do require the use of several cut-outs; three chariots, two designed with fire motifs and one with stars; a large star for Venus; and two salamanders. The Milkyway may result from leg drops, which may be withdrawn for the revelation of Juno. According to Simonson, one could expect such a spectacular setting to be accentuated through the use of fireworks in the Region of Fire.

Plate XIX

Setting. — Act IV, 10 - 13, The forecourt to the Palace of Venus. Again, the rolling clouds over the inner stage indicate the location of the deity machine which is not used for the entire setting. The five wings, again set diagonally to create an angular perspective toward the point of infinity, depict sculptured baroque figures and arches, embellished with little amorettoes (cf. III, 11). No shutters are extended in order that a great amount of clearance may be available for the large entrance of Scene 12.

Action. — With the establishment of the locale, Eufrosine, one of the Graces, appears beyond the forestage wings riding a turtle. The design for this action has not been supplied. Apparently the turtle moves quite slowly, requiring two whole Scenes, from the distant, deep stage to the front of the forestage, then off past the front wing, perhaps at stage right. Eufrosine sings a solo during the entire period.

Contrasting with the solo and slow movement of the preceding scenes, the action of Scene 12 introduces a triumphal pageant car onto the deep stage. The car is drawn by two lions, probably mechanical, and transports Mars and Venus at the head of a victory procession which moves quickly downstage following the exit of Eufrosine. On foot, before the lions, is Cecrops, together with captured

---

[6] Lee Simonson, *op. cit.,* 218. "This was a favourite stage-effect. It occurs in an interact dumb show of Peele's, *The Battle of Alcazar* (1589). 'The sky is on fire and the blazing star appears' recurs in *The Life and Death of Captain Thomas Stukeley,* and continues to be used into the seventeenth century. Elizabethans were adept in the use of fireworks, . . ."

and bound soldiers. The pageant car also bears such properties as military weapons, a sceptre, a crown, and the military dress of Juno and Pallas. On top of the car is Victory, a real character who holds the laurel crown over Mars and the golden apple over Venus. From the inner stage a chorus of soldiers follows in train.

The design of Burnacini illustrates a moment of Scene 13, when Cupid enters, flying from above the left middle stage down to the car. He is warning that the celebration has been made too soon, for the Athenians are besieging the fortress of Mars, thereby providing a cue for the next scene change.

Setting. — Except for an illusionary ball and chain, perhaps of wood and painted black, all the properties are adapted from earlier settings. The chief set piece is a genuine pageant wagon, useable for a Fasching street procession and decorated with twisted figure and motifs of the baroque period. The wagon is connected by harness to two mechanical lions, which could have been made with animal skins, hair, and masks and operated by two stagehands, respectively, making a total of four stagehands necessary.

Special effects. — The turtle, on which Eufrosine rides and sings during the opening scenes, probably requires an additional two stagehands for its operation. The materials obtainable for its composition could have been wood, clay, leather, and cloth. The baroque intent is to entertain the audience with very realistic animal appearances.

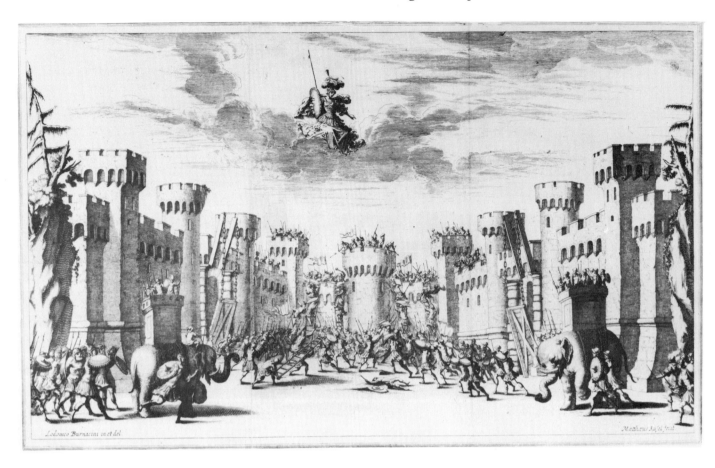

Plate XX

Setting. — Act IV, 14 - 15, as signaled by Cupid at the close of the last setting, shows the fortress of Mars. While the front wings, set horizontally, repeat the cliff and tree motif, used in Act III, Scenes 7 - 10, wings 2 - 4 are set diagonally to create the impression of a walled fortress with lookout towers. The fifth wing appears to be horizontal. A shutter with a built-out tower completes the setting at the end of the forestage. But the tower may be a separate, moveable unit. For the heavy action of this Scene sequence, the shutter-wall and tower require strong supports to hold them firm.

Action. — Athenians, led by Adrasto and Alceste, obey a trumpet sound and assault the stronghold. Elephants, probably mechanical, but realistic as were the lions and turtle, must be constructed sturdy enough to provide the support for two ensembles of attacking soldiers.[7] These rooks must be made equal in height to the size of the bastion attacked. Five ladders brought onto the main stage are moved against the bastion wall (first shutter). Defenders of the fortress, stationed on the other side, can be supported by ladders and scaffolding. The "dead" soldiers on the main stage can be carried offstage by their comrades at the close of the setting.

At the climax of the battle, Scene 15, Pallas appears in the sky, riding a chariot. This larger composition requires the use of the inner stage deity machine, as indicated by Burnacini.

---

[7] Live elephants perhaps could have been made available for the scenes, but the brevity and intensity of the action seem rather to recommend the construction of artificial elephants.

Properties. — All the properties for this Scene have been employed in previous scenes, except for the ladders. The ladders, wall, and tower must all be functional. The drawbridges appear to be painted on the wings; no movement or use of them is required by the text.

ACT V

Plate XXI

Setting. — Act V, 1 - 8, The Villa of Paris. A quiet, peaceful setting, using deep perspective with wings and shutter on the inner stage, this villa presentation prepares the audience for the sensational deity revelations which follow. The front wing is omitted from the design; the second wing repeats the forest motif of Act I, Scenes 6 - 10. The next three wings suggest large, palatial structures. The shutter on either side is slightly extended to create the impression of open-air enclosures, decorated with bannisters and arches. The contrast of light and dark areas imply that these extensions are not three dimensional, but are painted in perspective. The shutter at stage right also features a painted staircase, leading to a porch in the distance. The poplar trees are likewise painted details of the wings. But, attached to the shutter at stage right, Burnacini would like to have a three dimensional bannister, which encloses a three dimensional fountain. This problem was discussed earlier in relation to

Act I, Scene 15, where different possibilities were suggested, although the actual manner of staging was not resolved. Beyond the first shutter set, which follows the fifth wing and is indicated by a separation in the shadows, two inner stage wings are employed before another shutter closes off the set, as suggested by the use of light.

Action. — The Action of the scene sequence calls for a solo by Ennone in scene 1, followed by the arias of Filaura, Momus, and once more by Ennone, concluding Scene 2.

At Scene 3, darkened clouds gather above the inner stage. Whether this is accomplished by paint and masking or by raising and lowering of lights is not clear. Juno is revealed near the fourth forestage wing, followed by the revelation of Jupiter riding an eagle, probably a cut-out. He appears to fly slightly more toward the front of the stage in a manner that gives the scene to Juno. After a duet, Jupiter exits. The design of Burnacini appears to have condensed the action of Scenes 3 and 4 so that they probably could not be realized on the stage, should the production adhere strictly to the text. For in the Burnacini design Momus is singing his aria as Jupiter takes his leave of Juno and as a storm appears in the distance. According to the text, Jupiter exits at the end of Scene 3, a storm signals the start of Scene 4, and then Momus enters to comment on the coming events. In view of the directing complications, it seems unlikely that the design for Act V, Scenes 1-8, was ever realized on the Cortina stage.

Special effects. — As mentioned, Scene 4 is announced by a developing storm, complete with lightning and thunder effects. Ignited squibs could produce the former, and rolling drums could produce the latter. As the storm progresses, other special effects — rain and hail — are required. Traditionally, rain could be produced by pouring water through sieves, held by stagehands in the cloud machines or located on a grid above the main stage. Small paper or cloth wads could serve as hail. The cue for lightning is given by Juno, who sings *A' vendicarmi Turbini, e lampi,* to which Momus comments *Venga pur fiera tempesta . . . ;* and the Austrian nobility could readily comprehend that a fiery tempest was being staged.

The storm subsides, and Scenes 5-8 conclude the sequence as Ennone appears on stage to sing a solo, which takes all of Scene 5 before a climactic arrangement of arias sung by Aurindo, Filaura, and Momus is begun.

Plate XXII

Setting. — Act V, 9, as also Scene 10, is given independent treatment, using the full potential of the deep stage. The setting is the Piazza of Mars, with his palace in deep perspective (a painted shutter on the inner stage) and an isolated tower, which contains the golden apple, in the center (behind the fifth wing set). The wings of the forestage again depict cliff scenery, the motifs having been used as early as Act II, Scene 1. As the heaven opens (the inner stage deity machine), Jupiter is revealed, majestically enthroned and with eagles at his feet. Juno is at his side. Pallas and a large chorus fill two rows of the glorious revelation, which also includes various minor deities, played by the House of Habsburg.

Action. — A bolt of lightning (another squib), thrown by Jupiter, results in the destruction of the tower on the middle stage, concealing the golden apple. The eagles fly from his feet to the tower to retrieve the apple (probably accomplished by cut-outs and a concealed stagehand who could also manip-

ulate the destruction of the tower), and carry it to Jupiter. Venus, who sits on a chariot within the demolished tower, could also render the eagles a valuable assist before she culminates the Scene with her own return to heaven.

Special effect.—For true baroque effect, the tower would probably have been a collapsible, three dimensional, wood design carried onto the set by stagehands who left one of their members behind when they made their exit.

Plate XXIII

Setting and action.—Act V, 10, which concludes the performance, commences with a glory revelation, composed of a deity chorus which is led by Venus, Jupiter, and Pallas. At a cue sung by Jupiter, *Prima del auvenir si bella Imago,* a deep glory scene is discovered which exalts the House of Austria and Leopold I. In this grand finale, heaven and earth and sea are united in a ballet of the heavenly spirits: deities in heaven, nobility on earth in a large piazza surrounded by rich and superb edifices (the diagonally turned wings on the forestage) followed by a partially extended shutter, and sirens and tritons in the sea (inner stage). A seascape shutter at the farthest extent of the deep stage completes the distance perspective.

Special effects. — In the heart of the glory revelation is a painting, intended as a prophecy, with Leopold I and Margaretha in the center, surrounded by all the Habsburg ancestors and coming heirs. The brightness of the revelation was probably intensified by increasing the lamp glow and using mirrors to reflect light onto the painting of the royal pair.

The wings used for this set appear to be new, not having appeared elsewhere in the production. In all other respects, the Scene is a climactic summary of all the staging potential introduced throughout the opera.

To lend a finishing touch to the design, details of an eagle and flower pots are placed occasionally on top of the buildings.

Summary

With the preceding presentation and exposition of *Il pomo d'oro,* one may derive the following implications:

1. The *Theater auf der Cortina* may well have been the first continental building to employ a three-area stage in the attempt to bring scenery, action, and dialogue into one dynamic, spatial unity.

2. The areas of the Cortina stage were sometimes used in combination, such that the forestage was rarely used alone in *Il pomo d'oro* without some additional décor or set piece

before or within the first shutter-set area. The extent to which the inner stage was used depended on the designer's felt need for completing the distance perspective. Sometimes wings appear on the inner stage, but often an inner stage shutter suffices to complete the perspective.

3. The flying machines are usually shown above the third and fourth forestage wings, where two such machines appear frequently, and on the inner stage, where a deity machine is placed for apotheosis revelations. But the inner stage seems to have included one other flying apparatus, used in the Prologue. The construction of the apotheosis machine parallels those used in Venice, but the design of the second, smaller machine is quite uncertain.

4. The painting style was basically that of distance perspective, adopted from the renaissance, with innovations of baroque staging (two dimensional wings) and High Baroque designs related to spatial synthesis. The forestage wings at the Cortina in 1668 apparently could be turned to rest in a diagonal position.[8]

5. Wherever Burnacini deemed it fitting, wing scenery of cliffs, woods, and boats were repeated. This is particularly true for the front wings, the middle stage shutter, and the aquatic scenes on the middle stage. The scene of the inner stage shutter is not always clear, making the identification of repeated motifs difficult and uncertain.

6. Actors and actresses performed within the scenery.

7. However devious the means used for theatrical entertainment, the goal of the large operas at Vienna was political consolidation for the glory of the House of Habsburg.

[8] This precedent of Ludovico Burnacini, which had been credited by Francesco Galli-Bibiena to Andrea Pozzo and more recently to Troili because of his publication in 1672, has been noted in H. Kindermann, *op. cit.*, 341.

Part III:
Elaborations and Modifications

8

Influences of Ludovico Burnacini
in the German States

The impact of the festival creations by Giovanni and Ludovico Burnacini was quickly felt throughout the European continent. Ferdinand III had acquainted the nobility with the cultural force of High Baroque opera at the Regensburg Conference in 1653. His successor, Leopold I, enthusiastically promoted the creation of stages and the performance of High Baroque opera throughout the Holy Roman Empire, both in the Jesuit colleges and in the royal courts. Avancini, Sbarra, and Draghi were not merely poetic creators of librettos, they were literary leaders in a campaign to replace the Turkish influence in the East and the Swedish influence at Warsaw by the High Baroque ideology and culture from Vienna. The most outstanding *avant garde* element in this movement, however, was the engineering and scenic creativity of Ludovico Burnacini, whose rise to cultural leadership also helped to offset the influence of France and Torelli in the West.

Garden Theatres

As a designer of shows at Laxenburg, Schönbrunn, and the Favorita gardens, Ludovico Burnacini continued to elaborate the garden theatre movement which had become a favorite at Versailles, France. As his own contribution, Burnacini had made the Favorita Pond and its surroundings func-

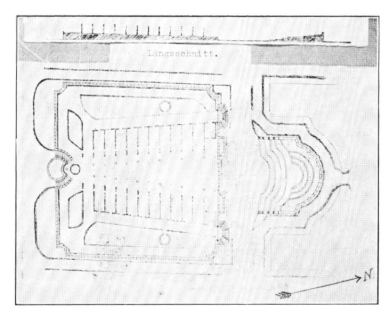

Figure 40A.   Open-air Theatre:
Plan of Herrenhausen Hedge-Theatre (reconstructed drawing of June, 1928, by Siedentopf, Surveying Director at Hanover).

Figure 40B.   A garden theatre at Salzdahlum near Wolfenbüttel, also in lower Saxony (engraving by J. J. Muller) R. Meyer.

tion as an integral part of the set. This concept of unified garden and theatre planning influenced many of the German states, but probably few approached the enthusiasm of Ulrich von Braunschweig and the Hohenzollerns for garden and theatre creations. The extent of this development in northern Germany is shown in Figure 40A and B, where the Burnacini innovations of deep staging and the seating arrangement at the Favorita seem to have left an impression at Herrenhausen and Wolfenbüttel.

Francesco Santurini

In the struggle to consolidate the Holy Roman Empire in western Europe, the art of the court opera also flourished at Munich, in Bavaria. The influence here, however, was more that of Giovanni Burnacini than of his son, Ludovico, during the latter decades of the seventeenth century. Following the triumphs of Giovanni Burnacini at Vienna (*La Gara*) and at Regensburg, Francesco Santurini was called from Venice to found a High Baroque opera movement at the aristocratic Bavarian court in Munich. Arriving in 1654, Santurini constructed a spacious opera house, in complete accordance with the Italian style, on the location of the one-time grain storage building at the Salvatorplatz in Munich, approximately opposite the present Ministry of Culture.[1] As with the first theatre structure of Giovanni Burnacini, the main feature of the elaborately detailed and gilded semi-circular auditorium was the duke's seat, decoratively covered and placed in the center. Three galleries were supported by ornate columns. The parterre was left open for tournament scenes and large ballets. The construction of Santurini was particularly significant as being perhaps the first theatre in the German states to be architecturally independent and free of material relation to the buildings of the palace. To the time of his death, 1682, he remained in the service of the Munich court twenty-eight years without interruption as the chief architect and stage designer.

As did Giovanni Burnacini, Santurini continued the development of the deep perspective principle, with symmetrically balanced wing-scenery. His designs are characteristic for their high degree of clarity. With the premier performance of his first opera at Munich, *L'Oronte,* Santurini acquired so much fame that no question concerning the author of the designs has ever arisen. For the most part, Santurini habitually employed eight pairs of wings. The elephant scene of Figure 41, indicates a possible influence from *Il pomo d'oro.*

On the forestage are two elephants, probably mechanical with movable trunks and similar in appearance to those used on the Cortina stage. The elephants would seem to be located between the proscenium arch and the first wings. Although an ensemble of soldiers and cavalry appear to be on a middle stage, they may simply have made an entrance between the third and fourth wings, or between the fourth and fifth wings, on an otherwise eight wing stage. The clouds in the distance suggest the availability of flying machines for *Berenice vendicativa.* The costuming is still very much traditional renaissance styling, as was the fashion in Viennese shows during the same period.

Johann Oswald Harms

As the Italian cultural invasion of Vienna had created a favorable atmosphere for the rise of Austrian composers, Schmelzer and Leopold I, and their notable successor, Joseph Fux, so the architectural innovations of Ludovico Burnacini may be considered to have aided the recognition of Johann Oswald Harms (1643 - 1708) as the first real German scene painter and theatre architect. Born in Hamburg, Harms worked in Dresden, Hanover, most definitely in Brunswick, and finally again in his home town. He was a designer of strong individuality, notwithstanding his great indebtedness to Ludovico Burnacini and the Venetian architects; and he was able to elevate German baroque opera, along with its near-relative of ballet, to a considerable height of cultural respectability. Heinz Kindermann estimates that if anyone had to select a designer of baroque scenes, derived from German origins, whose

---

[1] Kindermann, *op. cit.,* 340, 518 - 520.

Figure 41.   Design of Santurini for the opera *Berenice vendicativa* (Munich, 1680); elephant scene. Kindermann, *op. cit.*

talents would compare favorably with those of the Burnacinis and the Galli-Bibienas, then that designer was Harms.[2] His education was acquired in Rome, under Salvator Rosa. His transition from scholarly pursuits to art, as was being developed in the theatre and opera, expressed itself most strongly during his postgraduate days spent in Venice. After a visit to Vienna and a two-year employment at the ducal court of Saxony-Zeitz, Harms began his rise to fame at the Dresden Court in 1677. His position was that of "chief theatrical scene-painter" (*Hoff-und Ober Theatralischer Maler*).[3] In the reconstruction of the Dresden Comedy-house (1678-79), Harms played a significant role. But he was primarily famous there for producing his highly acclaimed *Ballet of the Conjunction and Effect of the Seven Planets on their Chosen Courses to Saxony,* which was so colorful and stylistically independent that the decorations have come to be regarded as the best characteristic expressions of the entire German baroque theatre movement. In the published edition of the text, nine of the eleven illustrations

[2] Kindermann, *op. cit.,* 542-547.

[3] Horst Richter, *Johann Oswald Harms,* Emsdetten (Westf.) Verlag Lechte, Bd. 58 Der Reihe *Die Schaubuhne,* 1963 sub- mitted originally as a dissertation to The University of Cologne, 13, 32. The purpose and character of Harms' visit to Vienna is still being researched.

Figure 42A.   Harms: Scene from the operatic ballet of the *Seven Planets* (1679): battle tents during the Turkish War. cf. Figure 42B. Garden and Revelation Scene.

included have been signed by J. O. Harms. Figure 42A and B presents a setting of tents and towers for the action of a battle against the Turks. *Deep staging of the sort introduced by Ludovico Burnacini appears to be used, with* seven wings on the *forestage,* a *middle stage* of sufficient size to accommodate large entrances and exits as well as flying machines and set pieces, *and an inner stage for additional wings and a large deity machine.*

A comparison of this scene with those of *Il pomo d'oro,* Act II, 10-12, and Act IV, 14-15 suggests an extensive indebtedness of Harms to L. O. Burnacini in matters of stage planning, action based on intersecting diagonals, costuming and properties, scene painting, and the use of heavy flying apparatuses on the middle- and inner stages. But equally evident is that J. O. Harms deviated considerably from Burnacini in the variety of tent designs, the increased number of persons in the ensembles, and use of much larger deity machines on the middle stage. A tendency away from precision in line and detail is also characteristic of Harms' technique, especially noticeable in his cloud designs.

Two other designs, placed together by Kindermann for comparison, further demonstrate the impact of L. O. Burnacini at the Dresden Court through the artistry of J. O. Harms (Figure 43A and B). The illustration at the top is also from *The Ballet of the Conjunction and Effect of the Seven Planets.*

Figure 42B.

Figure 43A.   Performances at Dresden. *Effect of the Seven Planets.* J. O. Harms.

Here the seven wings of the forestage are easily identifiable, and the use of shadows on the floor imply that the partially extended shutters are followed by another shutter on the inner stage. The apotheosis machine which appears to have Jupiter mounted on an eagle is strongly in the Venetian and Viennese tradition (*Il pomo d'oro,* Act V, 1 - 8, 9). The wing scenes show arches and twisted columns in the High Baroque manner cultivated by Burnacini. But, again, Harms moves away from line precision in favor of greater color and mass emphasis. The turban, as well as the make-up suggested for the two men at stage left, also indicates an interest in oriental motifs not previously evident in the works of High Baroque designers. A tendency toward simplicity of mass and line in the costumes which are essentially seventeenth century adaptations of Greek and Roman dress seems to be in evidence.

The illustration on page 126 reminds one that Ludovico Burnacini had designed many operas and ballets for the Hofburg Ballroom. Similarly, at Dresden, the *Ballet of the Moors,* illustrated by J. Azelt, was performed in the large salon of the residential palace. Although a date is not given for the performance, it is significant that such shows occurred at Dresden before 1650. In this case, no influence can be assigned to Ludovico Burnacini, since the performance antedates his work at Vienna; but it does point up his importance for the continuity of such salon shows in Europe. Whether the illustrated setting is a backdrop only, or a set consisting of nine wings and a shutter is not clear, since

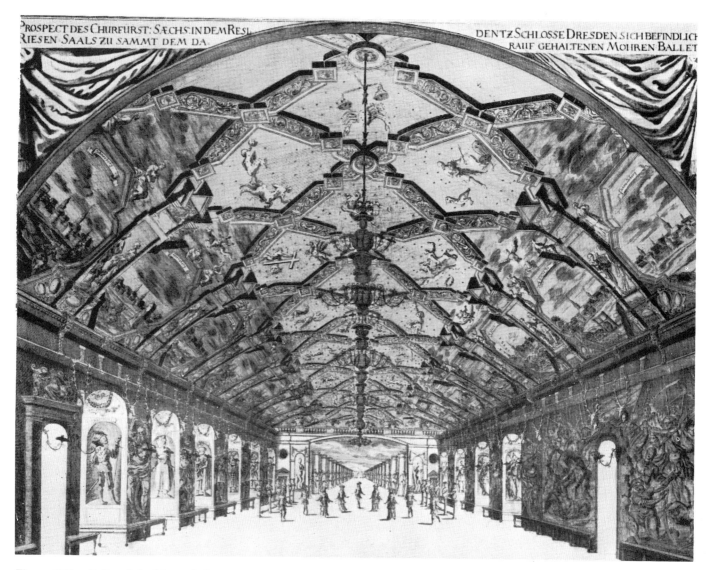

Figure 43B.   *Ballet of the Moors* (before 1650).

all the dancers are in front of the scenery. The costumes appear to be in Venetian Renaissance styling with oriental emblems and props.

In Harms' *Paris-Ballet* at Dresden, 1679, one striking scene, bearing marked resemblances to
Act I, Scenes 4-5, of *Il pomo d'oro,* is described as the Salon of the Gods, with a banquet for the
Olympian deities. Numerous clouds are made to move freely through the acting space. Depth is stressed
by means of a sequence of six cloud formations at the right and left of the stage floor, suggesting
the use of wings. On each cloud billow is seated a torch-bearing Satyr. From an entrance to the left
of the forestage, between the proscenium and first wing, comes a procession of Satyrs, servants in
classical Greek and Roman costumes, Amorettoes, pages, and servants of the court. All of them have
lovely properties, including colorful bowls, wine containers, and tableware. The procession moves
in a lengthy arch through the salon and returns to a second regally decorated room. In this second
room the Olympian gods are seated at a banquet table, placed on a slightly raised, semi-circular plat-
form. With its excessive heavy décor, this room appears to be a confusing, pompous picture of fan-

tasy. Its theatricalism, expressed through color and movement, is a high point of beauty for baroque scene painting.[4]

The unique quality of Harms, which sets his work apart from that of the Italian masters, lies in the precedence he assigns to painting, as opposed to previous emphasis on architectural styling. The Italian scene designers preferred the architecturally strict, systematic arrangement of depth divisions, but Harms prefers a color effect both in detail and for the whole set. As a rule, Harms achieves his grand effect with only four or five wing sets and a shutter, although the *Seven Planets* production is somewhat more elaborate. Between the third and fourth wings, and after the fifth wing, architectural columns are commonly built out in the form of a perspective arch. The inner stage consists of side-wings and a shutter with painted perspective. In the banquet scene, an arching staircase and banquet table, both functional, are introduced on the inner stage. The clouds used throughout the set are sometimes pendants and sometimes standing wings. But each billowing wing has its painted Satyr.

The cultivation of German ballet, which was transplanted from French soil, flourished as early as the first half of the seventeenth century in such towns as Stuttgart, Munich, Brunswick and Wolfenbüttel, and especially in Dresden. One of the earliest German ballet performances in the baroque period occurred at the Stuttgart Court in 1618. In a single remaining description of this outdoor performance, a floating island on a pond was reported, and the island was said to have had a Garden of Paradise. Through the center of the floating island an aisle extended, in the middle of which twelve knights, clothed in shining garments decorated with silver ornaments, sat grouped about a fountain. Behind them stood Neptune with his fork and the God of the Moors, who explained the significance of the concluding dance in German and French.

Following the Peace of Westphalia in 1648, the tradition of ballet, which had been interrupted by the Thirty Years' War, was revived. But this time the influence of opera made itself noticeable, altering the older ballet forms. At the Wolfenbüttel *Spring Ballet* of 1656 the beginning of an Act was often preceded by a vocal chorus with musical accompaniment. For the *Ballet of Nature* at Wolfenbüttel in 1660, many short vocal arrangements were introduced, which were more or less related to the story; e.g., an aquatic ballet was introduced by the fitting vocal accomplishments of Ulysses, his sailors and the Sirens. In the latter production, each scene was changed to the delighted eyes of the audience. The setting for the fourth part, which during the first half of the sequence showed the burning of Troy, was apparently changed to a large hell scene, complete with dragons, salamanders, and similar creatures.[5] It is in the midst of this tradition, yet towering above it, that Johann Oswald Harms stands with his *Planet Ballet.* This production also includes several vocal compositions. But the scenery is introduced with previously inexperienced movement. The music is probably that of Christoph Bernhard.[6]

In 1679, Harms was commissioned to design the operatic ballet, *Judicio Paridis and the Theft of Helen,* at Dresden. After 1686, he was the machine designer, chamber servant, and painter at the court of the luxury loving Duke Anton Ulrich von Braunschweig, who himself often directed performances, casting himself in a number of major roles. To the time of his death in 1708 Harms maintained his connection with the court at Brunswick, even though he had risen to greater fame in Hanover, where he assisted the construction of the opera house and designed productions for the same, in Celle, in Kassel, and after 1695 again in his home city of Hamburg. According to Horst Richter, many

---

[4] Horst Richter, *op. cit.,* 190-192, DE 12; cit. Kindermann, 543.

[5] Kindermann, *op. cit.,* 544.

[6] *Ibid.,* 546.

Figure 44. J. O. Harms: Hell-mouth for *Ixion,* performed in Brunswick, Germany, 1691. cf. Plate VIII of L. O. Burnacini, p. 97.

of the hundreds of remaining scene decorations from Harms state the exact location of the design; an equal number which may be presumed to have been intended for Brunswick and Hamburg are without reference to the performance location. Many of the illustrations are black-white designs; but, together with the testimony of persons who were in attendance at the shows, they suggest the emphasis which Harms gave to color effects.[7] To be sure, he was in all respects of staging, scene painting, and machinery deeply indebted to Ludovico Burnacini; yet as an independent experimenter Harms dared to break with the formalism of the Italians and French. He precedes Juvarra in the conscious introduction of asymmetrical sets, and he does not hesitate to add to this an arch extending diagonally across the stage. Harms is also credited with a complete revolution in the perspective flow of the wings, as in his forest with streamers. In this case, instead of streets being surrounded by forest wings, the forest wings are surrounded by a street procession, the wings being positioned near the middle of the stage. But Harms achieves one of his unique effects by almost overloading the stage areas with staircases, parts of old ruins, columns, caryatids, and flower pots.

The fact that Harms created an aesthetic impact on the audiences, in spite of his unusual painter's approach to design problems, may be attributed to the varying sizes of his wings, each of which he designed by himself. The wing sizes close to the point of distance, he felt, seemed to reduce too

[7] Horst Richter, *op. cit.,* 88. Even Leibniz, with his negative criticism of the performances during the Summer Fair of 1690, could not deny his admiration for the decorations of Harms, although he complained otherwise that a person would wonder whether for the price he had not rather have lent a helping hand to console the faithful, whose tears were crying to heaven. " . . . ob man mit ihren Preis nicht lieber hätte die Armen beschenken und die Gläubiger befriedigen sollen, deren Tränen zum Himmel schrien." Leibniz to the Landgrafen of Hessen-Rheinfels, Bd. II, 236 (Letter of September 14, 1690).

Figure 45A.   Scene 1

Figure 45B.   Scene 2

Figure 45A & B.   Lee Simonson, *Das Rheingold* (Metropolitan Opera Assn., New York: 1948)

strongly. In other words, Harms understood that he had to relate the dynamic elements of staging into an organic synthesis according to the requirements of German style, making possible a peculiarly German development.[8] When he placed trees, cliffs, or ships with wind-tossed sails on the stage, the intertwining of their convolutions as they appear to combine and grow together made a strong appeal to sense realism. Persons sympathetic to the views of Hans Tintelnot, Germany's leading authority on baroque art and theatre, have come to regard the designs of Harms as among the best artistic creations of the north German baroque culture.

The principal Italian designer whom Harms held in high esteem was Ludovico Burnacini. The preference of Harms for exotic and colossal effects is shared by numerous other baroque designers, including those in German districts. The technique by which the lines and masses dovetail in his wing scenes is probably the most significant contribution of J. O. Harms to the history of stage décor.

Twentieth Century Effects

An example of modern setting which emphasizes the more recent staging contributions of Adolphe Appia in continuity with the tradition extending back to Ludovico Burnacini is that of *Das Rheingold*, Scenes 1 - 2, designed by Lee Simonson and illustrated in Figures 45A and B.[9] Missing are the twisting contortions, caryatids, and statuesque details which characterized the High Baroque styling of Burnacini and Harms, but one still recognizes the balanced use of diagonal dimensions in restating and elaborating the motifs of the wings, cut-out drops, set pieces, and elevations. The winding staircases have been reduced to one expansive sequence of elevations, curved about the center of the fore- and middle stages. The traditional wood and water scenery has been simplified and altered to support rather than dominate the opera. On the deep stage, the use of the shutter has been replaced by a painted backdrop, but the perspective extending to a point of infinity is still evident in the first Scene. In the second Scene, the deep stage has been employed for the introduction of a suggested castle scene in a manner reminiscent of the Burnacini hell and harbor settings. If flying machines and glory apparatuses were employed, a person could almost imagine himself again attending an opera of a leading German town in the seventeenth century.

Summary

The influence of the Burnacinis did indeed spread rapidly throughout the German states. In part, this expansion and assimilation of High Baroque culture can be explained as a fulfillment of the desire to consolidate the peoples of central and eastern Europe in response to the challenges of the French, the Turks, and the Swedes. If this was not the real cause, it certainly was perceived as a desirable educational goal. The success of the Burnacinis and Avancini at the Imperial Court was quickly followed by the invitation and fame of Santurini in Munich. But the conclusion that High Baroque art

---

[8] *Ibid.,* 202. "Harms glich die barocke Bühnendekoration in sehr persönlicher Weise dem deutschen Stilgefühl an und ermöglichte eine deutsche Sonderentwicklung." Horst Richter compares the contributions of Harms to the influences of Inigo Jones in England and Jean Bérain in France.

[9] Lee Simonson, *op. cit.,* 154 - 155.

and theatre was fundamentally an Italian phenomenon does not follow. The infusion of Italian art into German society encouraged the development of a German baroque culture with its own peculiarities, based on the aesthetic interests of the people in different social contexts. The music of Sbarra and Cesti was certainly promoted at Vienna, Prague, and Warsaw, and their influence is evident in the Jesuit compositions of Schmelzer and Leopold I; but it is the concern of these latter for the cultivated development of German folk music which finds emphatic expression in the compositions of Joseph Fux, who created the accompaniments for the scenic displays of Francesco and Giuseppe Galli-Bibiena. Also to be noted is the fact that Joseph Fux, the first major composer at the Imperial Court under Karl VI, was not an Italian, but an Austrian.

Likewise, the impact of Ludovico Burnacini on German culture was certainly both intensive and extensive, as was that of Santurini in Munich. The immediate results of this impact have already been presented in the chapter on *Il pomo d'oro*. The further consequences of the Burnacini influence are evident in the high esteem which Johann Oswald Harms gave to his methods of staging, scene painting, and using machinery. Yet, the most important contribution which Ludovico Burnacini may be said to have made to German theatre was his stimulus to the independent activity of Harms which became evident in the shows at Dresden, Brunswick and Wolfenbüttel, Hanover, Celle, and Hamburg, as well as in the theatre plan for Hanover. The art of the Counter-Reformation had revitalized the wellsprings of the Reformation, preparing their flow into new channels of cultural activity.

9

Conclusion

Our principal concern throughout has been that of establishing the historical events responsible for the development of High Baroque opera at the Imperial Court in Vienna. The realization of this objective requires a constant awareness of theatre history within the context of cultural history under the Habsburgs.

More specifically, our aims have been to bring significant data into discussions on theatre history, written in English, to characterize the leadership and contributions of Ludovico Burnacini at the Imperial Court, to present a production analysis of *Il pomo d'oro* as a detailed example of the Burnacini methods and techniques, and to suggest the influence of Ludovico Burnacini's achievements toward the development of an independent movement in German High Baroque culture and theatre. To stress the complete cultural significance which was clearly a part of the most outstanding High Baroque performances, a separate treatment was given to Nicolaus Avancini and his works.

A methodological aim has been to demonstrate the practicability and desirability of a functional approach to theatre history, such as has been developed at The Ohio State University under the leadership of Professor John H. McDowell. By the presentation, identification, classification, and analysis of a typical performance with a view to actual stage production, it is hoped that a few problems may come nearer to resolution than would be the case by identification alone without any discussion of staging problems involved. The main illustration of this method has been the presentation and analysis of *Il pomo d'oro*. By the analyses here provided, it is felt that the superior quality of the functional method for treating problems in theatre history has been confirmed.

In order that a socio-historical basis might be supplied for understanding the conditions which helped to give rise to baroque art and culture, some space was given to developing comprehension of the transition from renaissance to baroque styling. Exploring the interrelationships of painting, sculpture, theatre, music, economics, social structure, and the anthropological ideals during the transition from the sixteenth to the seventeenth century, I dare to hope that a better foundation has been laid for identifying and explaining the specific ideas of High Baroque opera. The shift in painting and sculpture, we have noted, was marked by a tendency away from the renaissance concepts of horizontal lines and masses balanced toward a point of infinity to the more dynamic use of diagonals with curved, bulging masses in brilliant, contrasting colors directed toward a vertical synthesis, which characterized High Baroque art. In music, the change was marked by a transition from choir music and instrumental ensembles to the tonal murals of Gabrieli. Making their contribution to dynamic unity in theatre production, the designers of the baroque and High Baroque theatres realized many of the plastic art ideals on the stage through the development of the two dimensional wing and shutter set, the operation of a single machine to accomplish the *changement à vue,* the invention of a movable glory machine for apotheosis scenes, and the construction of the deep, functional three-area stage by Ludovico Burnacini. Again, the changes already mentioned would not have been really possible in southern and central Europe apart from the rise of the new financial centers following the Thirty Years' War. The displacement of Lübeck by Leipzig in the fur trade was an economic parable of the times. Many wealthy merchants began to feel that trade in tin, precious metals, and fine cloth might be more secure through the inland towns of Leipzig and Vienna than through the devastated and frequently besieged coastal towns.

The social structure was clearly delineated under the direction of the landed nobility and absolute monarchs who had risen to the position of political authority since the Reformation. At the *Theater auf der Cortina* the location of the duke's, viz. the emperor's, seat is evidently the chief point of perspective in the audience, about which other classes are ranked in order: the court, honored guests of the nobility and foreign ambassadors, high officials in the empire, wealthy bourgeoisie and suppliers of the court, and servants of the aristocracy. The vast segments of the common people, who had provided the inspiration and the original genius of baroque culture, were kept at a safe distance near the parterre entrances; but, more often than not they remained simply outside altogether. Relevant to the maintenance of the absolutist social order, the ideal character cultivated in baroque education was depicted as a man of elevated self-importance, obedient to a personal and divine will, insatiably curious, possessing great strength of memory, delighting in the real enjoyment of the senses, arrogantly awaiting public approbation, yet imaginative, courageous, and above all magnanimous. In terms of theatrical performances, these human attributes came to center in three leading themes: 1) Life is theatre; 2) the world is a stage, and wherever possible on the stage with great detail; 3) the prime mover and director of the world theatre is God, a personal and Divine Will.

Another leading concern of our study has been the special development of baroque theatre at the Viennese Imperial Court as traced from the reign of Ferdinand III to the early works of Ferdinando and Giuseppe Galli-Bibiena under Emperor Karl VI. Most significantly, we have discovered that the flourishing of High Baroque culture at the Imperial Court was a unified artistic enterprise of music, dance, and decoration. Some consideration was given to the construction of the Cesarea Corte, Regensburg, and Tummelplatz theatres, other places of performance, and descriptions of the more notable productions. With the treatment of Favorita Garden productions, the method of functional analysis was introduced for the tentative explanation of illustrated scenes. In this same connection, we have sought a greater appreciation of the monumental labors of Ludovico Burnacini in building the-atres, renovating salons and ballrooms, and designing garden theatres, not to mention the annual Fasching celebrations.

While writers on the history of the theatre have been prone to stress the contributions of the Bur-nacinis somewhat apart from related events at the Imperial Court and elsewhere in The Holy Roman Empire, I felt that a better understanding of the dramatic performances in the Viennese High Baroque period would be gained by bringing the work of the Burnacinis into association with that of Avancini, as often was in fact the case. By drawing this association one can acquire a clearer apprehension of the religio-political concern of the Habsburg emperor for the education of his citizens through the new art forms. The performances at the University of Vienna Aula were public shows, often attended by Leopold I, who was amply complimented by the service which these rather secular religious dramas gave to his glorious majesty. Through these shows the citizenry could also learn many of the most modern staging methods and techniques, which otherwise most of them would probably never see, due to the exclusive nature of the court productions.

The court productions had the same objectives as those at the university; viz., the cultivation of ideals felt to be most significant for the consolidation of the empire and the obedience of all social class-es to the divinely chosen ruler, Leopold I. Of course, many comedies were performed for light entertain-ment, but the most elaborate shows could be counted on to center a good bit of attention on the glory of the emperor. The responsibility for housing and designing the larger, aristocratic and private produc-tions was that of Giovanni Burnacini, and after him Ludovico Burnacini.

Under the leadership of the former, a unity of aesthetic enterprise was achieved at the Imperial Court. Musician, poet, and designer combined to create the first operatic extravaganzas, dedicated to the service of the emperor. To further this aesthetic unity, Giovanni Burnacini and his son erect-ed theatres at Vienna and Regensburg, the latter for the entertainment and instruction of a political conference. These theatres, which incidentally demonstrated an architectural effort to resolve prob-lems of aesthetic space through dynamic unity of scenery and action, contained the latest technolog-ical innovations in wing staging, machinery, and lighting. In other words, Ludovico Burnacini was able to acquire a first-hand acquaintance with the most recent ideas in architecture while he was still an adolescent.

Following the death of his father, Ludovico Burnacini strove to carry on the family tradition in architecture. In his first creative period, one notes very little independence from the designing tech-niques of the father, a matter that might well be explained by the financial straits in which the young Ludovico found himself continually. After 1659, however, both finances and art express a new spir-it of independence, and with the production of *Il pomo d'oro* (1668) Ludovico has already won acclaim as the leader of the post-Torelli generation. In matters of staging, his unique development of the inner stage from which the large apotheosis machine could be operated seemed to achieve the dynamic, uni-fied resolution of space that had been of so much concern to the baroque scene designers. His architec-tural accomplishments with the Cortina and the garden theatres also became so famous that his con-structions were considered ideal models for similar performance places erected throughout southern and central Europe for decades.

Il pomo d'oro is held to be an outstanding example of High Baroque synthesis in art and stage production. The text and scene designs from this festive opera have been treated in depth in order to attempt a demonstration of the most probable manner in which the new stage at the Cortina was em-ployed to resolve the problems in the staging of the opera. To offer a more complete exposition of the scene productions, costume descriptions were suggested for each sequence analyzed. The conclusions of the production analysis, found at the end of that chapter would only suffer from further repetition here.

Creativity such as that expressed in the works of Ludovico Burnacini could not help but have a most pervasive influence. We have witnessed the Burnacini influence in Munich and in the northern sections of the German states between Dresden and Hamburg. Nor did the Burnacini influence stop or evaporate during the rise of the Galli-Bibienas, who often put the innovations of Ludovico Burnacini to good use at the Favorita Gardens. A view of scenes from contemporary Wagnerian productions, designed by Lee Simonson, suggests that the concepts of Ludovico Burnacini are still very much alive, although improved technology and historical adaptation have brought about many alterations.

A large amount of research still needs to be done on the various influences of Viennese High Baroque culture throughout Europe, especially in connection with the achievements of Santurini and Harms. Until more individual studies are done on these and other personages responsible for High Baroque décor, the relationships between the High Baroque designs of Ludovico Burnacini and the Late Baroque productions of Giuseppe Galli-Bibiena cannot be soundly appreciated.

Bibliography

Reference Works

Dramatic Index. Boston: F. W. Taxon, Inc., G. K.Hall and Co., 1965.

Encyclopaedia Britannica. III, Henry A. Millan, "Baroque Architecture," 132-133D; William C. Fleming, "Baroque Art," 133-135D. XV, Sir Donald F. Tovey, "Monteverdi, Claudio," 762. XXII, Lee Simonson, "Theatre," part 1, historical development, 28-37; part 2, design and construction of modern theatres, 37-44. Chicago: Encyclopaedia Britannica, Inc.,1962.

Enciclopedia Dello Spettacolo. II, Joseph Gregor, "Burnacini," 1374-1378. V, Heinz Kindermann, "Germania e Austria," 1074-1099; Willi Flemming, "Gesuiti, Teatro dei," 1167-1170. Rome: Casa Editrice LeMaschere, 1954, 1958.

Larousse Encyclopedia of Renaissance and Baroque Art. General ed. René Huyghe. New York: Prometheus Press, 1964.

Loewenberg, Alfred. *Annals of Opera,* 1597-1940, An annotated bibliography of operas compiled from original sources. Genève: Societas Bibliographica, 1943.

The Oxford Companion to the Theatre. Phyllis Hartnoll, ed. London: Oxford University Press, 1951.

Sonneck, Oscar G. T. *Catalogue of Opera Librettos* printed before 1800, I-II. Washington, D.C.: Government Printing Office, 1914.

Books

Adler, Guido. *Denkmäler der Tonkunst in Österreich,* Jahrg. III/2-6; Marc Antonio Cesti, *Il Pomo D'Oro,* Graz: Akademische Druck- und Verlagsanstalt, 1896, 1959.

Alewyn, R. "Vom Geist des Barocktheaters," Weltliteratur *Festgabe fur Fritz Strich.* Bern: 1952.

Alt, Robert. *Bilderatlas zur Schul- und Erziehungs Geschichte,* I. Berlin: Volk und Wissen Volkseigener Verlag, 1960.

Altman, George *et al. Theatre Pictorial.* Berkeley, California: University of California Press, 1953.

Avancini, P. Nicolaus. *Pietas Victrix, sive Flavius Constantinus Magnus de Maxentio Tyranno Victor,* with 9 scene designs. Wien: owned by the Österreichischen Nationalbibliothek, 1659

Baker, Blanch M. *Theatre and Allied Arts.* New York: H. W. Wilson Company, 1952.

Baur Heinhold, Margarete. *Theater des Barock.* München: Verlag Georg D. W. Callwey, 1966.

Beyer, Guenther, and Beyer, K. *Barock.* Dresden: Sachsenverlag, 1961.

Biach-Schiffmann, Flora. *Giovanni und Ludovico Burnacini,* Theater und Feste am Wiener Hofe. Wien-Berlin: Krystall-Verlag, 1931. OSUTC film no. 123.

Bjurström, Per. *Giacomo Torelli and Baroque Stage Design.* Stockholm: Almquist and Wiksell, 1961.

Briggs, Martin S. *Baroque Architecture.* New York: McBride, Nast and Company, 1914.

Brinckmann, Albert E. *Die Baukunst des 17. und 18. Jahrhunderts,* "Barock-skulptur," Vol. 4, 1919. Berlin-Neubabelsberg: Akademische Verlagsgesellschaft Athenaion, m.b.h., 1915-22.

Burrough, Thomas H. B. *An Approach to Planning.* London: Pitman, 1953.

———. *South German Baroque.* London: A. Tiranti, 1956.

Castelfranco, Giorgio. *Leonardo da Vinci.* New York: Harry N. Abrams, Inc., 1960.

Cheney, Sheldon, *The Theatre:* Three Thousand Years of Drama, Acting and Stagecraft. New York: Longmans, Green, 1952.

Croce, Benedetto. *Aesthetic.* New York: The Noonday Press, 1960.

Damerine, G. "Monteverdi e la scenografia veneziana," *Scenario,* 3. Milano: 1934, 177-179.

D'Amico, Silvio. *Storia del Teatro Drammatico,* II. Milano: Garzanti Editore, 1958.

Davenport, Millia. *The Book of Costume,* I. New York: Crown Publishers, 1948.

Eisler, Max. *Historischer Atlas,* 16. Wien: Arbeiten des Kunsthistorisches Instituts der Universität Wien, n.d.

Flemming, Willi. *Deutsche Kultur im Zeitalter des Barock.* Potsdam: Akademische Verlagsgesellschaft Athenaion, 1931.

———. *Die Oper,* published in *Deutsche Literatur,* Reihe Barock, Barockdrama, 5.

———. *Oratorium Festspiel,* published in *Deutsche Literatur,* Reihe Barock, Barockdrama, 6. Leipzig: Verlag von Philipp Reclam, 1933.

———. *Das Ordensdrama,* published in *Deutsche Literatur,* Reihe Barock, Barockdrama, 2, with the complete text of *Pietas Victrix* by N. Avancini. Leipzig: Verlag von Philipp Reclam, 1930.

Freedley, George and Reeves, J. *A History of the Theatre,* rev. ed. New York: Crown Publishers, Inc., 1955.

Galli-Bibiena, Giuseppe. *Monumenta Scenica,* introduction by Joseph Gregor. Berkeley, California: Samuel J. Hume, Inc., 1954.

———. *Architectural and Perspective Designs,* introduction by A. Hyatt Mayor. New York: Dover Publications, 1964.

Grassi, Liliana, *Barocco e no.* Milano: Görlich, 1953.

Gregor, Joseph. *Geschichte des österreichischen Theaters.* Wien: Donau-Verlag, 1948.

———. *Weltgeschichte des Theaters.* Zürich: Phaidon Verlag, 1933.

———. *Wiener Szenische Kunst,* I-II. Wien: Amalthea-Verlag, 1925.

Grout, Donald Jay. *A Short History of Opera,* I. New York: Columbia University Press, 1947.

Haas, Robert. *Die Wiener Oper.* Wien-Budapest: Eligius Verlag, 1926.

Hager, Werner. *Die Bauten des deutschen Barocks.* Jena: E. Diederichs, 1942.

Hadamowsky, Franz. *Barocktheater am Wiener Kaiserhof,* mit einem Spielplan (1625-1740). Wien: Verlag A. Sexl, 1955.

Hartt, Frederick. *Sandro Botticelli.* New York: Harry N. Abrams, Inc., 1953.

Hausenstein, Wilhelm. *Die Kunst und die Gesellschaft.* München: R. Piper and Company, 1917.

———. *Vom Geist des Barock.* München: R. Piper, 1924.

Hauser, Arnold. *Mannerism,* I-III. London: Routledge and Kegan Paul, 1965.

Heaton, Herbert. *Economic History of Europe.* New York: Harper and Brothers, 1948.

Hewitt, Barnard. *The Renaissance Stage.* Coral Gables, Florida: University of Miami Press, 1958.

Hyatt, Mayor A. *The Bibiena Family.* New York: H. Bittner and Company, 1945.

Jellicoe, Geoffrey Alan. *Baroque Gardens of Austria.* London: E. Benn, Ltd., 1932; New York: C. Scribner's Sons, 1932.

Kann, Robert A. *The Habsburg Empire,* A Study in Integration and Disintegration. New York: Frederick A. Praeger, 1957.

———. *A Study in Austrian Intellectual History,* from Late Baroque to Romanticism. New York: Frederick A. Praeger, 1960.

Kernodle, George R. *From Art to Theatre.* Chicago: The University of Chicago Press, 1947.

Kindermann, Heinz. *Theatergeschichte Europas,* III-IV. Salzburg: Otto Müller Verlag, 1959.

Kinsky, George, ed. *A History of Music in Pictures.* London: J. M. Dent and Sons, Ltd., 1937.

6

Kitson, Michael. *The Age of Baroque.* New York: Mc-Graw-Hill, 1966.

Kralik, Heinrich. *The Vienna Opera,* trans. R. Rickett. London: Methuen and Company, Ltd., 1963.

Lang, Paul Henry. *Music in Western Civilization.* New York: W. W. Norton and Company, Inc., 1941.

Laver, James. *Drama Its Costume and Décor.* London: The Studio Publications, 1951.

Liess, Andreas. *Wiener Barockmusik.* Wien: Verlag L. Doblinger (B. Herzmansky), 1946.

McDowell, John H. *A Syllabus for History of the Theatre* (Speech 632, 633). Columbus, Ohio: The Ohio State University Theatre Collection, 1964, 1962.

Macgowan, Kenneth, and Melnitz, W. *The Living Stage.* Englewood Cliffs, New Jersey: Prentice-Hall, Inc., 1955.

Mantua, Fabricio Carini Motta. *Trattato sopra la struttura de' teatri e scene.* Guastallo: 1676.

Meyer, Rudolf. *Hecken u. Gartentheater in Deutschland im 17. 18. Jahrhundert, Emsdetten,* 1934.

Montagu, Lady Mary Wortley. *Letters and Works,* I. London: 1837.

Müller, Johannes. *Das Jesuitendrama,* I. Augsburg: Dr. Benno Filser Verlag, GMBH, 1930.

Newton, Eric. *European Painting and Sculpture.* Baltimore, Maryland: Penguin Books, 1962.

Nicoll, Allardyce. *The Development of the Theatre,* 4th ed. London: Harrap and Company, Ltd., 1958.

_____. *Masks, Mimes and Miracles.* New York: Cooper Square Publishers, Inc., 1963.

_____. *Stuart Masques and the Renaissance Stage.* New York: Benjamin Blom, Inc., 1963.

Niessen, Carl. *Das Bühnenbild,* 2nd ed. Bonn: Fritz Klopp Verlag, 1927.

Ornstein, Martha. *The Role of Scientific Societies in the Seventeenth Century.* Chicago, Illinois: The University of Chicago Press, 1938.

Pevsner, Nikolaus. *Barockmalerei in den romanischen Ländern,* 18. Wildpark-Potsdam: Akademische Verlagsgesellschaft Athenaion, 1928.

_____. *An Outline of European Architecture,* 6th ed. Baltimore, Maryland: Penguin Books, 1960.

_____. *Sir Christopher Wren.* New York: Universe Books, 1960.

Preclin, Edmond, and Tapié, V. L. *Le XVII siécle, monarchies centralisées.* Paris: Presses universitaires de France, 1943.

Priestly, J. B. *The Wonderful World of the Theatre.* New York: Garden City Books, 1959.

Richter, Horst. *Johann Oswald Harms, Ein deutscher Theaterdekorateur des Barock.* Emsdetten (Westf.): Verlag Lechte, 1963.

Rolland, Romain. *Histoire de l'opéra en Europe avant Lully et Scarlatti.* Paris: E. Thorin, 1895, 1931.

_____. *Some Musicians of Former Days,* trans. Mary Blaiklock. New York: Henry Holt and Company, 1915.

Sabbatini, Nicolo'. *Pratica di Fabrecar Scene e Machine ne' Teatri* (1638). Rome: Carlo Bestetti.

Scheid, N. "P. Nikolaus Avancini, S. J., Ein österreichischer Dichter des 17 Jahrhunderts," *Jahresbericht der Stella Matutina.* Feldkirch: 1898-99.

_____. "P. Nikolaus Avancini als Dramatiker," *Jahresbericht der Stella Matutina.* Feldkirch: 1912-13.

Schimmer, Gustav Adolph. *Das Alte Wien.* Wien: Verlag von L. C. Zamarski, Universitäts-Buchdruckerei, 1854.

Scholz, János. *Baroque and Romantic Stage Design.* New York: Beechhurst Press, 1950.

Schwarz, Johannes. *Die kaiserliche Sommerresidenz Favorita auf der* Wieden in Wien. Wien und Prague: 1899.

Sekler, Eduard F. *Wren and His Place in European Architecture.* New York: The Macmillan Company, 1956.

Simonson, Lee. *The Art of Scenic Design.* New York: Harper and Brothers, 1950.

_____. *The Stage is Set.* New York: Dover Publications, 1946.

Sitwell, Sacheverell. *A Background for Domenico Scarlatti.* London: Faber and Faber, Ltd., 1935.

_____. *Baroque and Rococo.* New York: G. P. Putnam's Sons, 1967.

_____. *German Baroque Art.* New York: G. H. Doran Company, 1928.

_____. *German Baroque Sculpture.* London: Duckworth, 1938.

_____. *Southern Baroque Art.* New York: A. A. Knopf, 1924, 1951.

Slosson, Preston, Hyma, and Boak. *The Growth of European Civilization.* New York: F. S. Crofts and Company, 1943.

Southern, Richard. *The Seven Ages of the Theatre.* New York: Hill and Wang, 1961.

Stamm, Rudolf, ed *Die Kunstformen des Barockzeitalters.* Edmund Stadler, "Die Raumgestaltung im Barockentheater," 190-226; Hans Tintelnot, "Zur Gewinnung unserer Barockbegriffe," 13-91. Bern: Francke Verlag, Sammlung Dalp, 1956.

Strakosch-Grassmann, Gustav. *Geschichte des öster-reichischen Unterrichtswesens.* Wien: Verlag von A. Pichlers Wittwe und Sohn, 1905.

Sypher, Wylie. *Four Stages of Renaissance Style.* Garden City, New York: Doubleday and Company, Inc., 1956.

Tapié, Victor Lucien. *The Age of Grandeur,* trans. A. Ross Williamson of *Baroque et Classicisme.* New York: Grove Press, 1960.

————. *Baroque et Classicisme.* Paris: Plon, 1957, 1961.

————. *Les États de la Maison d'Autriche de 1657 à 1790.* Paris: Centre de documentation universitaire, 1961.

Tintelnot, Hans. *Barocktheater und Barocke Kunst.* Berlin: Verlag Gebr. Mann, 1939.

Torrefranco, F. "Il primo scenografo del popolo G. Burnacini," *Scenario,* 3. Milano: 1934.

Vehse, E. *Memoirs of the Court and Aristocracy of Austria,* I-II, trans. Franz Demmler. London: H. S. Nichols, 1896.

Weilen, Alexander von. *Die Theater Wiens,* I-IV. Wien: Gesellschaft für Verfielfältigende Kunst, 1899-1906. OSUTC Film no. F21.

Weisbach, Werner, *Der Barock als Kunst der Gegenreformation.* Berlin: P. Cassirer, 1921.

————. *Die Kunst des Barock.* Berlin: Propyläen-verlag, 1926.

————. *Vom Geschmack und Seinen Wandlungen.* Basel: Amerbach-verlag, 1947.

Wellesz, Egon. *Essays on Opera,* trans. Patricia Kean. New York: Roy Publishers, 1950.

Wentinck, Charles. *El Greco.* New York: Barnes and Noble, Inc., 1964.

White, Eric Walter. *The Rise of English Opera.* New York: The Philosophical Library, 1951.

Wiel, T. *I teatri musicali veneziani del settecento.* Venezia: 1897.

Wittkower, Rudolf. *Art and Architecture in Italy: 1600-1750.* Baltimore, Md: Penguin Bks, Inc., 2nd rev. ed., 1965.

Wölfflin, Heinrich. *Renaissance and Baroque,* trans. Kathrin Simon. New York: Cornell University Press, 1966.

Wolf, Abraham. *A History of Science, Technology, and Philosophy in the 16th and 17th Centuries.* New York: The Macmillan Company, 1939.

Worsthorne, Simon T. *Venetian Opera in the Seventeenth Century.* Oxford: Clarendon Press, 1954.

Zucker, Paul. *Styles in Painting.* New York: Viking Press, 1950.

————. *Die Theaterdekoration des Barock.* Berlin: R. Kaemmerer, 1925.

Periodicals

Bielenberg, John E. "A Three-Dimensional Study of Two Scene Designs by Filippo Juvarra." *The Ohio State University Theatre Collection Bulletin,* 11 (1964), 6-20.

Morrow, John C. "O.S.U. Theatre Collection: A Unique Facility," *Players Magazine,* XLI, 2 (November, 1964), 57-58.

Warner, Fred E. "The Ottoboni Theatre." *The Ohio State University Theatre Collection Bulletin,* 11 (1964), 37-45.

West, William R. "Some Notes Concerning Staging at the Ottoboni Theatre Through an Analysis of Il Teodosia." *The Ohio State University Theatre Collection Bulletin,* 11 (1964), 21-34.

Newspapers

Corriere ordinario (Avvisi Italiani). Wien: 1677, 1678, 1685-1721. Nationalbibliothek.

Philemeri Irenici Elisii Diarium Europaeum, I-VI (January, 1657-February, 1661). Nationalbibliothek in Wien.

Relationis historicae semestralis continuatio Jacobi Franci (also "Frankfurter Relations"), Nrs. 39-102. Frankfurt am Main: Sigismundi Latomi, with Mäurers, Sel Erben, *et al.* Wien: Nationalbibliothek.

Theatrum Europaeum, or true description of all memorable events . . . Frankfurt am Main: Matthaeus Merian, 1-12 (1617-1685). Wien: Nationalbibliothek.

Wiennerisches Diarium. Wien: Joh. Peter von Ghelen, 1703-1740. Wien: Nationalbibliothek.

Document

600 Jahre Universität Wien. Wien und München: Österreichischer Bundesverlag für Unterricht, Wissenschaft und Kunst, 1965.

Films

The Ohio State University Theatre Collection.
   Opera Librettos:

La Gara	Vienna, 1652
Theti-Niobe	Mantua, 1652
L'Inganno d'Amore	Regensburg, 1653
La Zenobia	Venice, 1666
Il Pomo D'Oro	Vienna, 1668
Il Fuoco Eterno Custodito delle Vestali	Vienna, 1674
La Lanterna di Diogene	Vienna, 1674
Il Ratto delle Sabine	Vienna, 1674
Creso	Vienna, 1678
Sulpitia	Vienna, 1697
La Costanza d'Ulisse	Vienna, 1700

Columbus, Ohio: The Ohio State University Theatre
   Collection, 1967.

Special Collections

Musiksammlung der Albertina in Wien.
   Partitur   16011
                     164
                     371
                     406
                     407
                     744
                     762
                     874

Hajedecki, Alexander. *Sammlung* II, Convolut IV. Wien:
   Die Handschriftenabteilung der Nationalbibliothek, A - F, Testamentskopien.

Dissertations

Edwards, Homer F., Jr. *The Concept of Baroque in
   German, English, and French Scholarship.* An
   annotated bibliography, subdivided according
   to language and chronology; dealing mainly with
   architecture, sculpture, and painting. Emory University, 1964.

Lengl, G. *Die Genesis der Oper.* München: 1936.

Tauschhuber, G. *Kaiser Leopold und das Wiener
   Barocktheater.* München: 1947.

Index